Contents

Introduction

Refugees is Volume 284 in the **ISSUES** series. The aim of the series is to offer current, diverse information about important issues in our world, from a UK perspective.

ABOUT REFUGEES

There are many misconceptions and myths surrounding refugees, and yet their plight is an issue that affects people in every country around the globe. This book explores the difference between immigrants and refugees, looks at why people become refugees and considers what can be done to help people who find themselves in need of refuge in a foreign country. It also delves into the issues of statelessness, refugee camps and detention centres.

OUR SOURCES

Titles in the **ISSUES** series are designed to function as educational resource books, providing a balanced overview of a specific subject.

The information in our books is comprised of facts, articles and opinions from many different sources, including:

⇨ Newspaper reports and opinion pieces

⇨ Website factsheets

⇨ Magazine and journal articles

⇨ Statistics and surveys

⇨ Government reports

⇨ Literature from special interest groups

A NOTE ON CRITICAL EVALUATION

Because the information reprinted here is from a number of different sources, readers should bear in mind the origin of the text and whether the source is likely to have a particular bias when presenting information (or when conducting their research). It is hoped that, as you read about the many aspects of the issues explored in this book, you will critically evaluate the information presented.

It is important that you decide whether you are being presented with facts or opinions. Does the writer give a biased or unbiased report? If an opinion is being expressed, do you agree with the writer? Is there potential bias to the 'facts' or statistics behind an article?

ASSIGNMENTS

In the back of this book, you will find a selection of assignments designed to help you engage with the articles you have been reading and to explore your own opinions. Some tasks will take longer than others and there is a mixture of design, writing and research-based activities that you can complete alone or in a group.

FURTHER RESEARCH

At the end of each article we have listed its source and a website that you can visit if you would like to conduct your own research. Please remember to critically evaluate any sources that you consult and consider whether the information you are viewing is accurate and unbiased.

Useful weblinks

www.amnesty.org.uk

www.catholicherald.co.uk

blogs.channel4.com

www.channel4.com/news

www.theconversation.com

www.theguardian.com

www.handicap-international.org.uk

www.icrc.org

www.independent.co.uk

www.politics.co.uk

www.theprisma.co.uk

www.redcross.org.uk

www.refugeecouncil.org.uk

www.refugeesinternational.org

www.refugeewomen.co.uk

www.savethechildren.org

www.statelessness.eu

www.unhcr.org

Refugees

Series Editor: Cara Acred

Volume 284

Independence Educational Publishers

First published by Independence Educational Publishers

The Studio, High Green

Great Shelford

Cambridge CB22 5EG

England

© Independence 2015

Copyright

Photocopy licence

British Library Cataloguing in Publication Data

Refugees. -- (Issues ; 284)
1. Refugees--Great Britain. 2. Asylum, Right of--Great
Britain.
I. Series II. Acred, Cara editor.
362.8'7'0941-dc23

ISBN-13: 9781861687166

Printed in Great Britain
Zenith Print Group

Chapter 1

Refugees & asylum

Facts and figures about refugees

Who is a refugee?

A refugee is legally defined as a person who is outside his or her country of nationality and is unable to return due to a well-founded fear of persecution because of his or her race, religion, nationality, political opinion, or membership in a particular social group. By receiving refugee status, individuals are guaranteed protection of their basic human rights, and cannot be forced to return to a country where they fear persecution.

In 2014, there were 19.5 million refugees around the world, including 5.1 million Palestinian refugees. According to the UN Refugee Agency, the leading countries of origin for refugees in 2014 were:

⇨ Syria: 3.88 million

⇨ Afghanistan: 2.59 million

⇨ Somalia: 1.1 million

Find more refugee statistics from the UN Refugee Agency (http://www.unhcr.org/556725e69.html).

Who is an internally displaced person (IDP)?

Internally displaced people (IDPs) have been forced to leave their homes as a result of armed conflict, generalised violence, or human rights violations, but unlike refugees they have not crossed an international border. Although internally displaced people outnumber refugees by more than two to one, no single UN or other international agency has responsibility for responding to internal displacement. As a result,

the global response to the needs of IDPs is often ineffective.

In 2014, there were an estimated 38 million people displaced internally by conflict. The largest populations of internally displaced people are found in:

⇨ Syria: 7.6 million

⇨ Colombia: 6 million

⇨ Iraq: 3.4 million

⇨ Sudan: 3.1 million

⇨ Democratic Republic of Congo: 2.8 million.

Find more statistics from the Internal Displacement Monitoring Centre (http://www.internal-displacement.org/publications/2015/global-overview-2015-people-internally-displaced-by-conflict-and-violence).

Who is a stateless person?

Stateless people are individuals who do not have a legal bond of nationality with any state, including people who have never acquired citizenship of their birth country or who have lost their citizenship and have no claim to citizenship of another state. Children of stateless people often are born into statelessness and few manage to escape that status. According to the 1954 Convention relating to the Status of Stateless Persons, a *de jure* stateless person is someone 'not considered as a national by any State under the operation of its law.' Persons are considered *de facto* stateless if they have an ineffective nationality, cannot prove they are legally stateless, or if one or more countries dispute their

citizenship. The Office of the UN High Commissioner for Refugees (UNHCR) has the international mandate for responding to the needs of stateless people and leading the global effort to reduce statelessness. Historically, however, the agency has devoted few resources to this aspect of its mandate.

There are an estimated ten million stateless people around the world. Refugees International focuses its efforts on reducing statelessness, particularly for the following populations:

⇨ Syria: more than 300,000 denationalised Kurds

⇨ Kuwait: 93,000 Bidoon

⇨ Dominican Republic: an estimated 900,000 to 1.2 million undocumented individuals of Haitian origin, many of who are stateless or at risk of statelessness.

Read more about Refugees International work for stateless people (http://refugeesinternational.org/what-we-do/statelessness).

What is an asylum seeker?

An asylum seeker is a person who is seeking to be recognised as a refugee, but has not yet received formal refugee status. During 2013, some 1.1 million individual applications for asylum or refugee status were submitted to governments and UNHCR offices. With 109,600 asylum claims, Germany was for the first time since 1999 the world's largest recipient of new individual applications, followed by the United States of America (84,400) and South Africa (70,000).

Can a country refuse to admit refugees?

Under international law, refugees must not be forced back to the countries they have fled. This principle of non-refoulement is the key provision of the 1951 UN Refugee Convention, which defines international law and guidelines to protect refugees. Host governments are primarily responsible for protecting refugees and most states fulfil their obligations to do so. Others, however, avoid their responsibility by pointing to a lack of resources, threats to national security, fears of domestic political destabilisation, or the arrival of even greater numbers of refugees. This is a violation of international law that is binding on all states.

Learn more about the 1951 Refugee Convention (http://www.unhcr.org/cgi-bin/texis/vtx/home/opendocPDFViewer.)

⇨ The above information is reprinted with kind permission from Refugees International. Please visit www.refugeesinternational.org for further information.

Refugee FAQs

On asylum seekers and refugees in the UK

1. What are the main reasons that people become refugees, and what other reasons drive people from their homes and across borders?

There are many reasons. But a refugee is always someone facing persecution in his or her country of origin/nationality for one of five reasons – these include political opinion, religion and race. Normally, those forced to move by natural disaster are not refugees, though in the popular media, this term is often used to describe such people. Those fleeing from a civil war may also not be refugees if none of the specific reasons applies to the undoubtedly very serious harms that they are at risk of in their country of origin/nationality.

2. Is seeking asylum legal?

While it is lawful to seek asylum, an asylum seeker may need to break immigration laws to get to another country to make an asylum claim. The UK, will not normally accept asylum claims from outside the UK. Its immigration laws require most migrants to obtain permission before travelling to the UK. There are some exceptions to this, but those countries from where permission is not required to travel to the UK, tend to be countries from which someone is unlikely to need or want to seek asylum – e.g. Australia, Canada, USA, etc. The UN Refugee Convention requires that a State should not penalise refugees for having to cross borders in breach of immigration laws in order to seek asylum.

3. What's the difference between an asylum seeker and a refugee?

An asylum seeker is someone asking for asylum, asking another country that is not their country of origin/nationality, to permit them to live and receive the protection of that other country. A refugee is someone who is outside their country of origin/nationality and is at risk of persecution if returned to that country, as defined more fully by the UN Refugee Convention. In the UK, most refugees are people who are either seeking asylum or have sought asylum and then formally been recognised as being refugees. Many asylum seekers are refugees, of whom in due course the UK Home Office should recognise their status as refugees and grant them asylum.

4. Are the terms refugee and asylum seeker mutually exclusive?

May an asylum seeker who is waiting for their asylum application to be processed also be a refugee? The terms are not mutually exclusive. A person is a refugee by virtue of meeting the UN Refugee Convention definition. Subject to the provisions of that Convention they should be granted asylum. A refugee, therefore, may seek asylum (i.e. ask that another country, e.g. the UK, formally recognises his or her refugee status). Thus, the UK does not (and cannot) give or refuse refugee status. It does operate a system to determine whether someone is or is not a refugee and if accepting the person is a refugee it usually provides them an immigration status permitting them to live in the UK (refugee leave). It does not thereby grant refugee status. Rather it acknowledges its international obligations to the refugee and grants a UK immigration status to reflect those obligations.

5. If someone's asylum application is not approved, what are they?

If someone is refused asylum, they are just that – a person refused asylum. In some cases, the refusal is incorrect and the person remains a refugee but is yet to be recognised as having that status. Those refused asylum usually are permitted to appeal within the UK. They continue to be treated as asylum seekers unless and until their appeal is finally decided. If the appeal is dismissed, they will be treated differently – as refused asylum seekers – though in some cases, a refused asylum seeker may once again become treated as an asylum seeker if he or she makes a fresh asylum claim setting out new material or information to establish their entitlement to asylum.

6. How come asylum seekers and refugees get priority access to housing and benefits, i.e. get put above British people on the council housing list

They do not. Asylum seekers do not have access to council housing or to social security benefits. If an asylum seeker is recognised to be a refugee, they will be granted refugee leave (permission to remain in the UK) and then may be entitled to council housing and/ or social security benefits on the basis of the very same criteria as British citizens. Asylum seekers, whose asylum claims or appeals remain outstanding, can (if they would otherwise be destitute and homeless) receive accommodation and support from the Home Office at rates substantially below that for social security. Most asylum seekers access this support because they are not permitted to work in the UK, so cannot support themselves. Refused asylum seekers may be entitled to some support from the Home Office if they are for the time being unable to return to their country of origin/ nationality.

7. Do refugees and asylum seekers have the right to work in the UK?

Asylum seekers are normally refused permission to work in the UK. They may be permitted to take work if they have been waiting for more than a year for a decision on their asylum claim (i.e. the decision by the Home Office before any appeal). This is now very rare. If an asylum seeker is recognised to be a refugee, and granted permission to remain in the UK, then he or she will be free to work like any British citizen.

On refugees

8. What percentage of refugees are able to return home?

A refugee is someone who cannot return home safely. If someone is no longer at risk of persecution in his or her country of origin/nationality, he or she ceases to be a refugee. However, this does not mean it will be appropriate to expect them to return home. Much will depend upon what has happened in the intervening period – how settled have they become in the country in which they have sought asylum (e.g. the UK), to what could they return in their country of origin/nationality.

Consider: their family may now be settled in the UK, they may have established a new family in the UK, and they may have no family or community left to return to.

9. How do refugee children get access to education and schooling in the UK?

The UN Refugee Convention includes that refugees should have the same access to elementary education as citizens of the country in which they have sought refuge. As regards all other education, it says that refugees should have at least as good access (including as regards remission of fees) as the most favoured foreign nationals in that country. In the UK, education up to age 18 years is available to all children regardless of immigration status, so child asylum seekers up to this point should have access to education provided by a local authority. In practice, older children sometimes face bureaucratic difficulties, especially where a school is not properly aware of its obligations. Some local authorities provide alternative projects for children while they are waiting to find a school place. However, refugees may have difficulty accessing higher education (or post-18 further education) – either because it is not clear whether they will be in the UK to complete a course, or because they cannot afford a fee and cannot obtain a fee exemption. Once a refugee is formally recognised by the Home Office to be a refugee, these difficulties should be resolved. Someone granted refugee leave (the immigration status given to a refugee once the UK has acknowledged the person to be a refugee) should be treated as a home student, so may be eligible for any fee remission on the same basis of the same criteria as a home student. In some circumstances, other asylum seekers may also be eligible to be treated as a home student – e.g. if they have not been recognised to be refugees, but have been granted permission to remain in the UK for an extended period such as may happen when someone is at risk of serious harm if returned to his or her country of origin/nationality but not

for one of the five specific reasons relating to refugees.

10. What difficulties are faced by refugees in seeking asylum in the UK etc.?

There are many difficulties, and some may be greater for some refugees than others. Many refugees have suffered traumatic experiences. They may have been tortured, they may have suffered during their journeys to the UK (e.g. think of those who have survived when boats have sunk in the Mediterranean), or they may have become separated from family and not have any news about family members or witnessed family members being killed. Many refugees also find the system and their treatment in the UK to be traumatising, being isolated, not familiar with the culture or language, being asked to retell their story repeatedly – including traumatic events, being 'dispersed', being detained, being racially abused, or being unable to work or fill their days with meaningful occupation. Thus, many refugees (including after they have been recognised to be refugees and granted permission to remain in the UK) suffer significant mental health difficulties. Refugees also have difficulty getting good immigration advice and representation. This is particularly problematic because poor advice or representation may cause their asylum claim to be refused, and lead to them being detained and facing being returned to the country where they face persecution. Dispersal can exacerbate some of these problems. Refugees are not normally allowed to work unless and until their refugee status has been formally recognised by the Home Office. Hence, most refugees must rely upon the Home Office to provide accommodation and some financial support. Home Office accommodation is provided in different parts of the country, and while they are still seeking asylum refugees may be moved to accommodation far from friends, community, lawyers and other supporters (including healthcare

providers). This experience is for many quite disorientating. As for financial support, this is provided at far below the level of social security benefits provided to British citizens (the basic rate for otherwise destitute asylum seekers is just over £5 per day). Some refugees find themselves homeless and destitute; and some are or become vulnerable to labour or sexual exploitation.

On refugees and migrants

11. How does the treatment of irregular migrants and regular migrants differ?

A regular migrant in the UK is someone permitted to be in the UK. There may be conditions on that permission, and it may only last for a limited period of time. For so long as the migrant keeps to any conditions and while his or her permission (called leave) continues, the migrant is free to remain in the UK.

An irregular migrant has no permission to be in the UK. Unless they are able to regularise their status (i.e. become a regular migrant by applying for permission to be in the UK), they may be detained or removed from the UK. The irregular migrant will also be subject to laws, which mean they cannot be lawfully employed in the UK and an employer may be fined if employing them. The Government has recently passed laws to extend these sorts of difficulties so that some landlords may be fined for providing accommodation to irregular migrants. There have also been proposals to extend the healthcare charging these migrants face; and more recently to extend the penalties that landlords may face.

12. Can refugees be regular or irregular migrants?

Some refugees will be regular migrants and some will be irregular migrants. 'Regular' here simply refers to whether a migrant is complying with domestic immigration laws – so in the UK, if the person needs a permission (e.g.

a visa) to travel to the UK do they have permission? And if they need permission to remain in the UK have they got permission? There may be conditions on any permission that a migrant may have been granted, about whether they are permitted to work or not or how long they are permitted to stay in the UK. Most refugees cannot obtain permission to travel to the UK, but nonetheless must arrive here before they can make an asylum claim. Most of them (virtually all) come from countries for which a visa (a form of permission) is required before travelling to the UK. Therefore, most refugees travel to the UK as irregular migrants and claim asylum having entered the country. Some refugees are resettled to the UK.

In 2014, the UK resettled a small number of Syrian refugees. It also has a relatively small programme with UNHCR to resettle refugees from elsewhere in the world in the UK. Resettled refugees are agreed to be taken by the UK before they arrive here or travel to the UK. So they are regular migrants. Some refugees may also qualify to migrate to the UK as students or to work. They may never even seek asylum, because they have an alternative regular migrants' route to escape from persecution – though if the period for which they are permitted to be in the UK comes to an end and the risk to them continues – they may then need to seek asylum.

13. Are refugees treated differently to other irregular migrants?

Remember that some refugees will be regular migrants. For the many refugees that travel and/or arrive in the UK as irregular migrants, they are in a different position to other irregular migrants. The UN Refugee Convention provides that they should not be penalised for having broken immigration laws in order to seek asylum. In the UK, there is a specific defence in criminal law relating to breaches of immigration law, which is intended to protect refugees from prosecution. However, the Convention does not provide a blanket protection for any refugee to breach immigration laws – it merely seeks to ensure that immigration laws are not used to prevent or penalise the refugee who needs to breach these laws in order to obtain asylum. Even so, there have been several instances in recent years where refugees have been wrongly prosecuted and convicted of immigration – related offences despite this protection. This remains a serious concern.

On Amnesty International's work with refugees

14. What is Amnesty doing to help refugees in the UK?

Since 2006, Amnesty has joined together in a coalition of organisations campaigning to end destitution among asylum seekers and those refused asylum (including those who have been wrongly refused – e.g. because they received poor legal advice or representation). This coalition is called Still Human Still Here. More information about Still Human Still Here is available at: http://stillhumanstillhere. wordpress.com/. Over the last decade, Amnesty has conducted and published research relating to detention, destitution and poor quality decision-making on refugees' asylum claims. Some general information about Amnesty International UK's work relating to refugees is available at: http:// www.amnesty.org.uk/refugee- asylum seeker-migranthuman- rights.

⇨ The above information has been reprinted with kind permission from Amnesty International UK. Please visit www.amnesty.org. uk for further information.

© Amnesty International UK 2015

Top ten global facts about refugees

Today [18 June 2015] the UN's Refugee Agency UNHCR have published their annual analysis of global forced displacement, revealing shocking numbers of people who have been forced to flee their homes.

Here are the top ten stand out facts:

1. In 2014, global displacement reached historic levels: 59.5 million people were forced to flee their homes: roughly the same number of people as in Britain. If these people made up their own country, it would be the 24th largest nation in the world.

2. In 2014 alone, 8.3 million people were forced to flee: the highest annual increase on record.

3. That means that 42,500 people were forced to leave their homes every day because of conflict or persecution.

4. Of these people, 19.5 million are refugees, 1.8 million are asylum seekers and 38.2 million were internally displaced within their own country.

5. 86% of the world's refugees are hosted by developing countries.

6. Britain is home to just 0.6% of the world's refugees.

7. More than half (53%) of the world's refugees are from just three countries: Syria, Afghanistan and Somalia. The largest source of the world's refugees is Syria. One in five displaced persons is from Syria.

8. The top five host countries for refugees are:

⇨ Turkey

⇨ Pakistan

⇨ Lebanon

⇨ Iran

⇨ Ethiopia.

9. More than half of the world's refugees are children (51%): the highest figure in over a decade.

10. In 2014, 34,300 asylum claims were made by unaccompanied children: the highest number since records began. Most of the children were Afghan, Eritrean, Syrian or Somali.

Read the full report here: http://unhcr.org/556725e69.html#_ga=1.88197213.716588722.1426003938

18 June 2015

⇨ The above information has been reprinted with kind permission from the Refugee Council. Please visit www.refugeecouncil.org.uk for further information.

© 2015 Refugee Council

Housing refugees

More than 350,000 migrants have arrived at the EU's borders so far this year from conflict zones in Syria and Afghanistan as well as African countries like Eritea.

Would you agree to take a refugee into your home for six months?

11% Yes

14% Don't know

75% No

To what extent do you support or oppose your local council area housing ten refugee families?

16% Strongly support	**25%** Tend to support	**18%** Tend to oppose	**30%** Strongly oppose	**12%** Don't know

Source: One in ten Britons say they'd take a refugee into their home, YouGov, 3 September 2015

Asylum trends 2014

Levels and trends in industrialised countries

+36%
Among regions in Europe, an overall increase of 36% in annual asylum levels was reported by the five Nordic countries which received 106,200 asylum requests during 2014. The increase was particularly significant in Sweden (+38%) and Denmark (+96%). Reporting the second highest level on record with 75,100 asylum applications, Sweden was the main destination country accounting for 70% of all new claims registered in this region.

714,300
Europe received 714,300 claims, an increase of 47% compared to 2013 (485,000 claims).

+45%
An estimated 866,000 asylum applications were recorded in 2014, some 269,400 claims more than the year before (+45%). This is the fourth consecutive annual increase and the second highest annual level since the early 1980s. As such, the 2014 figure is close to the all-time high of almost 900,000 asylum applications recorded among the 44 industrialised countries in 1992.

11,700 → 9,000
The reported number of new asylum-seekers in Australia dropped by 24 per cent during 2014 (9,000 claims) compared to the previous year (11,700). In New Zealand, 290 asylum applications were registered in 2014

149,600
The Syrian Arab Republic remained the main country of origin of asylum-seekers in industrialized countries. Provisional data indicate that some 149,600 Syrians requested refugee status in 2014, more than double the number of 2013 (56,300 claims) and 17 times more than in 2011 (8,700 claims). The 2014 level is the highest number recorded by a single group among the industrialised countries since 1992.

+44%
The 28 Member States of the European Union (EU) registered 570,800 asylum claims in 2014, a 44% increase compared to 2013 (396,700).
EU States together accounted for 80% of all new asylum claims submitted in Europe.
Germany and Sweden accounted for 30 and 13% of asylum claims in the EU, respectively.

95%
In Southern Europe, the number of newly registered asylum seekers went up sharply to reach 170,700, the highest on record (+95%). Turkey and Italy were the main recipients of asylum applications in the region (87,800 and 63,700, respectively).

173,000
With 173,000 new asylum applications registered during 2014, Germany continued to be the largest single recipient of new asylum claims among the group of industrialized countries.

7,900
Japan registered 5,000 asylum applications in 2014 while the Republic of Korea recorded 2,900 claims. Although it is the highest level on record in both countries, numbers continue to be modest in comparison with other industrialised countries.

+42%
In North America, an estimated 134,600 new asylum applications were submitted in 2014, an increase of 42% compared to 2013 (94,800 claims).
Canada registered 13,500 new applications, about one third more than in 2013 (10,400), while the United States of America recorded approximately 121,200 claims, 36,800 claims more than in 2013 (+44%).

Global refugee figure passes 50 million for first time since Second World War

UNHCR report says more than half of those displaced are children, with aid organisations reaching breaking point.

By Harriet Sherwood

The number of people forced to flee their homes across the world has exceeded 50 million for the first time since the Second World War, an exponential rise that is stretching host countries and aid organisations to breaking point, according to figures released on Friday.

Half the world's refugees are children, many travelling alone or in groups in a desperate quest for sanctuary, and often falling into the clutches of people traffickers, the annual UN High Commissioner for Refugees (UNHCR) global trends report said.

More than 25,000 unaccompanied children lodged asylum applications in 77 countries last year, a fraction of the number of displaced minors across the globe.

'We are witnessing a quantum leap in forced displacement in the world,' António Guterres, head of the UN's refugee agency, said as figures for 2013 showed a total of 51.2 million refugees, asylum seekers and internally displaced people. If displaced people had their own country it would be the 24th most populous in the world.

The increase of six million over the 2012 figures has mainly been driven by the war in Syria. By the end of last year, 2.5 million Syrians had fled across the country's borders and 6.5 million were internally displaced – more than 40% of the population.

Conflicts in the Central African Republic and South Sudan also contributed to rising numbers.

The data represented 'a world where peace is dangerously in deficit', said Guterres. 'And that peace deficit represents the incapacity of the international community firstly to prevent conflicts and secondly, to find solutions to those conflicts.'

Some conflicts were unpredictable, but in other cases 'there are situations you see coming, but nothing is done to avoid the conflict'. He cited the 'enormous risks' in Nigeria as an example, adding that 'the international community has shown very little capacity to do something useful to prevent it from getting worse and more dangerous'.

Humanitarian organisations could only mitigate the impact of conflict on ordinary people. 'There is no humanitarian solution… The solution is political and the solution is to solve the conflicts that generate these dramatic levels of displacement.'

Factors that forced people to leave their homes included climate change, population growth, urbanisation, food insecurity and water scarcity – many of which interacted with and enhanced each other.

'It's sometimes difficult to identify the main motivation,' said Guterres, adding that movement could be due to several factors.

'The classic idea that you have economic migrants who want a better life, and refugees who flee conflict and persecution – it is true, but now you have a number of people who are forced to move by a combination of reasons, which are not always obvious.'

The number of forcibly displaced people in 2013 exceeded the populations of countries such as South Africa, Spain or South Korea, the UNHCR reported. An average of 32,200 individuals were forced to flee their homes each day.

It defined three groups:

⇨ Refugees – 16.7 million people worldwide. Apart from five million Palestinians, the biggest refugee populations by source country are Afghans, Syrians and Somalis, which together account for half the total. The main host countries were Pakistan, Iran, Lebanon, Jordan and Turkey. 86 per cent of the world's refugees are hosted by developing countries – up from 70% a decade ago.

⇨ Asylum seekers – close to 1.2 million people submitted asylum claims, mostly in developed countries. In terms of country of origin, the highest number was from Syria (64,300), followed by the Democratic Republic of Congo (60,400) and Burma

(57,400). Germany was the largest recipient.

⇨ Internally displaced people – a record 33.3 million were forced to flee their homes but remained within their country's borders.

Many of those crossing borders fell into the hands of increasingly sophisticated people-trafficking gangs, said Guterres. 'We see these networks of trafficking and smuggling becoming more and more international, multinational, and linked to other forms of international criminality', such as guns and drugs.

'They become very powerful organisations. And the truth is that national authorities, especially in the developing world… have a very limited capacity to crack down on them.'

At the same time, he added, 'their behaviour has become more and more vicious'. Gangs used rape, torture, sexual exploitation, organ harvesting, extortion and murder. 'We are very strongly in favour of international cooperation to crack down on these gangsters,' he said.

The scale of the refugee crisis was straining the capacity of humanitarian organisations, said Guterres. UNHCR has halved the proportion of its budget spent on headquarters costs, but there was an increasing gap between needs and resources available.

'Because conflicts are multiplying, because of climate change and other factors, we see the needs are increasing exponentially.'

The UN's world food programme had been forced to reduce rations in some refugee camps because of reduced budgets and greater demands, he said. 'Humanitarian organisations are under tremendous stress.'

20 June 2014

⇨ The above information has been reprinted with kind permission from *The Guardian*. Please visit www.theguardian.com for further information.

Refugees: the myths and the fears

By Lindsey Hilsum

I've received more abuse on Twitter while covering the refugee and migrant crisis in Europe than any other story I've reported. That's made me wonder about the potency of certain myths and fears that anger and worry a lot of people. So let me try to clear up some confusion.

1. 'They're not refugees. They're economic migrants.'

In the last three weeks on the road in Europe, about 80 per cent of those I've met have been Syrians. I've also met Iraqis, Afghans, Bangladeshis, Pakistanis and Senegalese. The Syrians are fleeing war – no question. Bangladeshis and Senegalese are probably in search of a better life because of poverty and lack of opportunity at home. With others it's more complex. Continuing conflict in parts of Afghanistan and Iraq has made normal life impossible for many, but definitions blur. If you're a young man whose father was killed in a car bomb in Baghdad and who cannot find work to support your mother and sisters, are you a refugee or an economic migrant? I'm not sure.

2. 'They're lying. They're not really Syrians.'

Certainly the best nationality if you want to be accepted as a refugee now is Syrian. I suspect that some of those who told me they were Syrian may have been Iraqi. But I am not an idiot. I ask people where exactly in Syria they are from and chat about what's happening there to see what they say. A translator has been helping me to distinguish Arabic accents. And when someone tells me he's from war-torn Somalia and gives me a Nigerian name, then I know he's lying.

3. 'They pay thousands to people smugglers. This proves they're not genuine refugees.'

You don't have to be poor to fear Islamic State or President Bashar al Assad's barrel bombs. Even rich people flee war. Many of the Syrians fleeing now are middle-class, English-speaking and university educated, but after five years of war life has become impossible. Globalisation means that many have relatives abroad who send money by Western Union or other transfer services. The Eritrean diaspora is particularly well organised. This distinguishes the current refugee crisis from previous ones.

4. 'Refugees stay in the first 'safe' country they reach. If they leave they become economic migrants.'

Under the Dublin Protocol refugees should claim asylum in the first EU country they reach. Nowadays that usually means Greece or Italy. Neither can cope, so Greece just lets people through. This is not the fault of refugees but it's true that most want to get to Germany or Sweden, where they may have relatives and where they know their children have a better chance of education and they may get work. Syria's neighbours – Jordan, Lebanon and Turkey – cannot cope with the four million Syrian refugees they're hosting. Refugee families who had hoped that by now the war would be over and they could go back to their old lives in Aleppo or Idlib realise that's not possible, but if they stay where they are their children will not go to school. They'll live forever in camps or building sites with no hope of a future. So they move. So would you. They're still fleeing war. This is why UNHCR has asked European and other countries to accept more refugees from camps in neighbouring countries, as Britain is now doing.

5. 'They'll be a burden on European societies.'

Initially, yes, it costs money to house and feed refugees. But refugees and migrants are often the most dynamic members of society. George Soros, for example. Or Einstein. I suspect one reason Germany is so open to Syrian refugees is because their society is ageing (like ours) so an injection of young, determined, often well-educated refugees might be quite helpful.

6. 'They're coming for the benefits.'

They're coming because they want a future. Statistically, after an initial period of settling in, refugees and migrants are less likely to claim benefits than natives.

7. 'They're all men, which proves they're not genuine refugees. They should fight for their country.'

Many of the 'economic migrants' are young men who hope to get a job and send home money to their families. Remittances to Africa are more significant than economic aid. Amongst refugees I've seen groups of young men as well as families. It's a mix. Some young Syrian men are fleeing conscription into Bashar al Assad's army. Others are disillusioned with the rebels. There are more than 2000 militia, including local groups, in Syria now. Joining one is not going to solve Syria's problems. It's entirely rational to flee not fight. (And men often take the dangerous journey alone hoping to get their families over separately later via a more safe route.)

8. 'Terrorists are infiltrating Europe by posing as refugees.'

Actually it's the other way round. European terrorists are going to Syria. If terrorists want to infiltrate Europe why bother to send them on a long, arduous journey? There are plenty of potential terrorists to recruit in Europe. Much cheaper and more efficient.

9. 'You show pictures of cute children to pull our heartstrings.'

Guilty as charged. Part of our job as journalists is to show viewers how this feels. I've seen hundreds of kids on this journey and I find it incredibly affecting. The girl watching Macedonia speed by from the train window as her exhausted family slept around her. The smiling toddler whose mother had placed him in a luggage cart at Vienna station. The little boy at the Austrian border who forgot all his tiredness and fear because someone had given him a plastic brontosaurus. We have an instinctively sympathetic response to children because they're necessary for the survival of the human race.

If we didn't have empathy we'd have died out long ago. The story of humanity is a story of movement, migration, birth and adaptation. This is just a tiny chapter.

7 September 2015

⇨ The above information is reprinted with kind permission from Channel 4 News. Please visit blogs.channel4.com for further information.

© Channel 4 2015

Stateless people

What is statelessness?

To understand how a person can lack a nationality, it helps to know how nationality works in practice. In simple terms, you acquire a nationality automatically at birth or you obtain one later on in life. Those who acquire nationality at birth do so because they were born in a country that gives nationality through birth on their territory (*jus soli*) or because their parents were able to transmit their nationality to their children (*jus sanguinis*), which usually applies regardless of where the child was born. Sometimes, however, people need to apply to become a national of a country and base their application on years of residence or a family link with the given country.

The international legal definition of a stateless person is set out in Article 1 of the 1954 Convention relating to the Status of Stateless Persons, which defines a stateless person as 'a person who is not considered as a national by any State under the operation of its law'. This means that a stateless person is someone who does not have a nationality of any country. Some people are born stateless, while others become stateless over the course of their lives.

Stateless people

People are often asked, at some point in their lives, what nationality they have. However, not many question how and why they have acquired their nationality. Is nationality something we are born with? Is it something we acquire? Can we lose it? The answer to these questions is yes. However, unless you have encountered problems with your nationality, you probably take it for granted.

Having a nationality is something so natural that people rarely stop to think about what life would be like without it. But at least ten million people worldwide have no nationality. That is the same as the combined populations of Norway and Denmark. Moreover, most of these ten million people are stateless by no fault of their own. Statelessness – not having a nationality – occurs because of discrimination against certain groups; redrawing of borders; and gaps in nationality laws.

The constant in all of this is that someone without a nationality cannot live the same life as someone with a nationality:

⇨ Try to get an ID card if you have no nationality;

⇨ Try opening a bank account without an ID card;

⇨ Try to board a flight without a passport;

⇨ Try to enrol in university without proof of nationality.

These things are impossible for stateless people to do in a way that is safe and dignified. So imagine a lifetime of obstacles and disappointment and imagine ten million people who cannot achieve their full potential. To help make a difference, support UNHCR's ten-year campaign to eradicate statelessness by the year 2024.

Cause of statelessness

One major cause of statelessness is the existence of gaps in a country's legal regime relating to nationality. Every country has a law, or laws, which establish under what circumstances one acquires nationality or can have it withdrawn. If nationality laws are not carefully written and correctly applied, some people can be excluded and left stateless. An age-old example is children found in a country who are of unknown parentage (foundlings). If nationality can only be acquired based on descent from a national, these children can be left stateless. Fortunately, most nationality laws avoid this and recognise them as nationals of the state in which they are found.

Another factor that makes matters more complicated is that many people move from the countries where they were born. Unless a country of origin permits a parent to pass on nationality through family ties, then a child born in a foreign country risks becoming stateless if that country does not permit nationality based on birth in the territory alone. Finally, the rules setting out who can and who cannot transmit their nationality are sometimes discriminatory. The laws in 27 countries do not let women pass on their nationality, while some countries limit citizenship to people of certain races and ethnicities.

A second important reason that statelessness occurs is the emergence of new states and changes in borders. In many cases, specific groups may be left without a nationality as a result of these changes. Even where new countries would allow nationality for all within the territory, ethnic, racial and religious minorities frequently have trouble proving their link to the country. In countries where nationality is only acquired by descent from a national (*jus sanguinis*), then this means that statelessness will be passed on to the next generation.

Statelessness can also be caused by a loss or deprivation of nationality. In some countries, citizens can lose their nationality simply from having lived outside their country for too long. States can also arbitrarily deprive citizens of their nationality through changes in law that leave whole populations stateless, using discriminatory criteria like ethnicity or race to define who and who does not belong to a state.

Is statelessness a problem?

Statelessness is sometimes referred to as an invisible problem because stateless people often remain unseen and unheard. And this makes it hard to show others how difficult their lives can be. A photograph of a stateless person may not make you cry, but knowing something about their lives might help you understand their suffering.

Imagine taking a sick child to hospital and being asked for an ID card to fill out a form that will allow them treatment. Imagine your shame and desperation at not being able to provide one. Imagine how sick you feel when you realise that your child is suffering because he has no nationality, no ID, no papers and the reason why is because you are a woman and were not allowed to give your child your nationality. This is the reality of a day in the life of a family affected by statelessness.

If you have no nationality, you often forfeit the basic rights that citizens enjoy – access to education and the job market, ability to buy and sell property or to open a bank account. When thousands of people are stateless for the same reason, this creates communities that are alienated and powerless. Over time, stateless communities have been pushed further into the margins of society where their situation is marked by constant sadness, frustration, depression and loss of a life in which they could have achieved much more. In the worst cases, statelessness can spill over into conflict and cause displacement.

UNHCR's Campaign to End Statelessness within ten years, launched in November 2014, aims to spread awareness about the issue, change perceptions about statelessness and push for action to resolve the problem once and for all. The campaign allows people like you to show solidarity with stateless people and put pressure on governments to change their laws and policies to ensure that everyone has a place in this world, so that everyone can say #IBELONG.

⇨ The above information has been reprinted with kind permission from United Nations High Commissioner for Refugees (UNHCR). Please visit www.unhcr.org for further information.

Refugees and displaced persons protected under international humanitarian law

Refugees are people who have crossed an international frontier and are at risk or have been victims of persecution in their country of origin. Internally displaced persons (IDPs), on the other hand, have not crossed an international frontier, but have, for whatever reason, also fled their homes.

Refugee law – mainly the 1951 Convention Relating to the Status of Refugees and the Convention Governing the Specific Aspects of Refugee Problems in Africa – and the mandate of the Office of the United Nations High Commissioner for Refugees (UNHCR) provide the main framework for protection and assistance for refugees. Refugees are also protected by general human rights law, and if they find themselves in a State involved in armed conflict, by international humanitarian law (IHL).

The general provisions of IHL protect civilian refugees in States involved in armed conflict, but they also receive special protection under the Fourth Geneva Convention and Additional Protocol I. This additional protection recognises the vulnerability of refugees as aliens in the hands of a party to a conflict.

Internally Displaced Persons

There is no convention for IDPs equivalent to the 1951 Refugee Convention. Nonetheless, international law protects persons from displacement and once they are displaced under several bodies of law:

⇨ IDPs are protected by international human rights law and domestic law;

⇨ In situations of armed conflict, they are protected by IHL;

⇨ The Guiding Principles on Internal Displacement, which are based on these two bodies of law, provide useful guidance on displacement-specific aspects.

Under IHL, people are protected from and during displacement as civilians, provided they do not take a direct part in hostilities.

IHL plays an important part in preventing displacement in the first place. It prohibits the displacement of people except if it is necessary for imperative military reasons or the protection of the civilians themselves. A widespread or systematic policy of displacement of civilians without such justification constitutes a crime against humanity.

Several rules of IHL protect the civilian population and their violation often constitutes a root cause of displacement. For instance, attacks by parties to an armed conflict on civilians and civilian objects are forbidden, as are indiscriminate methods of warfare that may have an adverse impact on civilians. Other rules whose respect will prevent displacement include the prohibition of acts that threaten the civilian population's ability to survive, such as destruction, without valid military reason, of crops, health facilities, water and power supplies or dwellings.

Collective punishment of civilian populations is also outlawed under IHL.

Humanitarian relief

International humanitarian law guarantees access for relief and humanitarian organisations to refugees and IDPs in situations of armed conflict. Parties to a conflict must facilitate the supply of relief materials such as medicines, food, blankets and tents.

Regrettably these rules have been ignored in many recent conflicts putting both refugee populations and IDPs in danger. The ICRC has consistently called on States and non-State armed groups to respect and ensure respect for international law and the basic principles of humanity when dealing with civilians. Only through respect of the rules of armed conflict can refugee flows and internal displacement be prevented; similarly, if people have to leave their homes, they can only be protected if IHL is complied with.

29 October 2010

⇨ The above information has been reprinted with kind permission from the International Committee of the Red Cross (ICRC). Please visit www.icrc.org for further information.

Immigration detention in the UK

This briefing provides an overview of immigration detention in the UK. It discusses the size of the UK's detention facilities, the number of detainees, the average duration of detention, and the detention of children.

By Stephanie J. Silverman and Ruchi Hajela

Key points

⇨ The UK immigration detention estate is one of the largest in Europe. From 2009 until the end of 2013, between 2,000 and 3,500 migrants have been in detention at any given time.

⇨ Around 30,000 persons entered detention in 2013 compared to approximately 29,000 persons in 2012.

⇨ The majority of immigration detainees are held for less than two months.

⇨ The single most common category of immigration detainees is people who have sought asylum in the UK at some point.

⇨ Over 1,000 children were detained for the purpose of immigration control in 2009, and this number was reduced to just under 130 in 2011. It rose to 240 in 2012, before falling to 228 in 2013 with the majority detained at the Cedars pre-departure accommodation facility, opened in September 2011.

⇨ In late 2014 the estimated average cost of detention was £97 per day.

Understanding the evidence

Immigration detention refers to the government practice of detaining asylum seekers and other migrants for administrative purposes, typically to establish their identities, or to facilitate their immigration claims resolution and/or their removals.

The reasons for which a migrant may be held in detention include: to effect removal; to establish a person's identity or basis of claim; where there is reason to believe that the person will fail to comply with any conditions attached to the grant of temporary admission or release, i.e. a risk of absconding; where there is a risk of harm to the migrant or the public; and as part of the detained fast-track (DFT) system (whereby asylum seekers could be detained if their claims appeared straightforward and capable of being decided quickly). There are also occasions when the reasons for a migrant's detention change while he or she is already being held in detention.

Border officials in the UK may detain migrants: on arrival; upon presentation to an immigration office within the country; during a check-in with immigration officials; once a decision to remove has been issued; and after a prison sentence or following arrest by a police officer.

The publicly available data on immigration detention chiefly originate in publications released by the Home Office and Her Majesty's Inspectorate of Prisons (HMIP). Data and information from non-governmental organisations' reports, Hansard texts of Parliamentary debates and formal questions and scholarly articles supplement this information.

The UK's immigration detention facilities are among the largest in Europe: between 2,000 and 3,500 migrants are detained at any given time

The UK has one of the largest networks of immigration detention facilities in Europe. After the repurposing of the Morton Hall prison as an immigration removal centre (IRC) in June 2011 and the opening of a short-term holding facility at Larne House in Northern Ireland in July 2011, UK detention capacity expanded to approximately 3,500 places. Over the past five years there have been between 2,000 and 3,500 migrants detained at any given time. As a snapshot example, just under 3,400 non-citizens were detained in UK facilities as of 30 September 2014.

Approximately 30,400 migrants entered detention in the UK in 2013

Approximately 30,400 migrants entered detention under Immigration Act powers in 2013, compared to 29,000 in 2012 and 27,000 in 2011 (UK Home Office 2014). These statistics do not include persons detained in police cells, Prison Service establishments, short-term holding rooms at ports and airports (for less than 24 hours), and those detained under both criminal and immigration powers and their dependents. Immigration detainees are held in Immigration Removal Centres (IRCs), Residential and Non Residential Short Term Holding Facilities (STHFs), and Holding Rooms either based at or near ports of entry and reporting centres.

As of January 2015, there were 11 IRCs, 4 RSTHFs, 1 NRSTHF, 1 pre-departure accommodation (for families), 19 Holding rooms at ports and 11 at reporting centres. Except for 4 IRCs that are managed by the Prison Service, the Home Office has outsourced the management of its detention facilities to private firms – Mitie, GEO, G4S and Serco. The contract for managing the Holding rooms, the NRSTHF and two of the four RSTHFs passed to Reliance (now Tascor) in 2011. Immigration detainees may also be detained in prisons and there is currently capacity for 600 detainees under a service level agreement with the National Offender Management Service.

Over half of immigration detainees are held for less than two months

In 2013, about 81% of total immigration detainees leaving detention had been held for less than two months. It is also not uncommon for detention to span two to four months. A small but consistent minority of detainees – about 6% – are held for more than six months, including 1% held for more than a year.

The most common category of immigration detention is people who have sought asylum in the UK at some point in their immigration adjudication processes

There are numerous categories of people who are detained under Immigration Act powers, and these categories can overlap. For example, new arrivals may be detained awaiting examination by an immigration officer to determine their right to entry; new arrivals who have been refused permission to enter the UK and are awaiting removal may also be detained; those who have either failed to leave the UK on expiry of their visas (so-called overstayers), have not complied with the terms of their visas, or have attained their visas by deception, may be detained; and undocumented persons found in the UK can be detained pending a decision on whether they are to be removed or pending arrangements for their removal.

The largest category of immigration detainees is persons who have sought asylum at some stage during their immigration processes. In 2013, asylum detainees accounted for about 60% of the total immigration detainee population (UK Home Office 2014). The Government's announcement in 2005 that it would process 30% of new asylum applicants through the detained fast track (DFT) system has contributed to the high numbers of asylum seekers in detention.

The immigration detainee population also includes foreign national offenders (FNOs), some of whom apply for asylum while in prison. Since April 2006, the UK Government has prioritised the removal of FNOs. As of 1 August 2008, with the introduction of the UK Borders Act 2007, all FNOs who have been sentenced to a period of imprisonment of 12 months or more are subject to automatic deportation from the UK unless they fall within one of the Act's six exceptions. Prior to removal, FNOs who do not qualify for an exception remain in prison under immigration powers and are not counted in official detention estate statistics. Since 2009, more than 4,000 FNOs have been deported annually. (See our briefing on 'Deportations, Removals and Voluntary Departures from the UK'.) In February 2010, foreign national offenders were detained for an average of 143 days; by January 2011 this had increased to 190 days, an increase of 33% (Vine, 2011). As at 30 September 2012, there were 828 FNOs in detention (UK Home Office 2013). Automatic deportation, however, does not preclude appeal rights.

The policy primer on 'Immigration Detention: Policy Challenges' provides more context, explanation and analysis of Foreign national offenders and asylum seekers in UK immigration detention.

Detention of children in 2013 was much lower than the 2009 levels

Throughout the 1990s, the Home Office rarely detained families with children. However, non-governmental organisations and other groups estimate the number of children detained with their families to have been up to 2,000 per annum between 2005 and 2009 (Sankey et al. 2010). Home Office statistics suggest that more than 1,100 children entered detention in 2009. This number fell to 436 in 2010 and to 127 in 2011. (Home Office 2014). In 2012 and 2013 the numbers increased to over 200 annually, including 228 children entering immigration detention in

2013. The majority were detained at the Cedars pre-departure accommodation facility.

To deal with family cases without detaining children, on 1 March 2011 the Government announced a new family returns process, having closed the family unit at Yarl's Wood IRC in December 2010. The new process includes: a Family Returns Panel to consider child welfare issues in families who refuse to leave; a family conference to discuss future options and the specific option of assisted return; the opening of Cedars in September 2011; and the expansion and refurbishment of Tinsley House IRC at London Gatwick airport. Both Cedars and Tinsley House hold families for up to 72 hours and require a ministerial declaration for extending a family's stay up to a week in exceptional cases.

With thanks to Mary Bosworth, Emma Kaufman and officials at the Home Office.

References

Crawley, H. (2011). *Detention by another name?* Migration Pulse, Migrants Rights Network, London, updated March 21 2011.

Hansard. *Detention of Children (UK Border Agency).* House of Commons Hansard debates for 14 December 2009 (pt 0001), House of Commons, London, 2009.

Hansard. *Immigration: Detention* by Lord Avebury. Lord Hansard text for 29 June 2011 (HL10229). House of Commons, London, 2011.

Her Majesty's Chief Inspectorate of Prisons. *Index of Immigration Removal Centre Inspections.* Inspectorate Reports, HMI Prisons, London, 2011.

Home Office. *Control of Immigration: Quarterly statistical summary first quarter 2011.* Home Office, London, 2011.

Home Office. *User Guide to Home Office immigration Statistics.* Home Office, London, 2011.

Home Office. *Children entering detention held solely under Immigration Act powers.* Home Office, London, 2012.

Home Office. *Foreign National Offenders in detention and leaving detention.* Home Office, London, 2013.

Home Office. *Immigration Statistics July-September 2014.* Home Office, London, 2014a.

House of Commons Home Affairs Committee. *The Detention of Children in the Immigration System.* First Report of Session 2009 – 2010, Vol. HC 73, House of Commons, London, 2009:14.

The Information Centre about Asylum and Refugees in the UK. *Detention of Asylum Seekers in the UK.* Thematic Briefing prepared for the Independent Asylum Commission, ICAR, Runnymede Trust, London, 2007:25.

Sankey, I., S. Farthing, and A. Coles. *Liberty's Submission to the Review into Ending the Detention of Children for Immigration Purposes.* Liberty, London, 2010.

Vine, J. *A Thematic Inspection of How the UK Border Agency Manages Foreign National Prisoners.* UK Border Agency (pp. 3, pp. 19), London, 2011.

UK Border Agency, *Enforcement Instructions and Guidance, Chapter 45 – Family cases.* Home Office, London, updated 25 April 2012.

6 February 2015

⇨ The above information has been reprinted with kind permission from the Migration Observatory. Please visit www.gov.uk for further information.

© *Migration Observatory 2015*

Syria: hardship, hope and resettlement refugees from Syria tell their stories

Amnesty International met with refugees from Syria in Lebanon, Jordan and Iraq. They spoke of loss, uncertainty, hardships, hopes and dreams. These are their stories.

Nadia, like many of the refugees from Syria that Amnesty International has interviewed, dreams of a better future for herself and especially for her teenage son. She is one of four million refugees who have fled Syria as a result of the ongoing brutal conflict, which has claimed the lives of over 190,000 people and broken apart homes, families, livelihoods and any sense of a normal life. Her son is now one of the 1.7 million refugee children from Syria at risk of becoming a 'lost generation'. He, like many other young refugees, struggles to attend school and lives in difficult conditions. 'School is very far. My son goes by bus. Sometimes I don't even have the money for him to take a bus so he stays at home. We are very poor. Sometimes we don't have anything to eat,' Nadia told Amnesty International.

While the sheer number of those displaced by the four-year crisis is astounding, it doesn't reflect the full impact the conflict is having on the people affected by it. Behind every number is a face, a name, a person who has experienced deep loss and who hopes for a better future.

This briefing highlights the stories of eight families and individuals from Syria who have escaped the conflict. They are based on interviews carried out by Amnesty International in Lebanon, Jordan and Iraq from October to December 2014. While the stories have been shortened to make them more accessible to the reader, the events recounted and statements made

are all told in their own words. Due to their extreme vulnerability and the harsh living conditions they face, the refugees interviewed here need to be resettled to another safe country outside of the immediate region.

Yara, a Syrian woman with four children who sought safety in Lebanon, told Amnesty International, 'My son's health situation is deteriorating and I would really like to treat him. The UN has put me forward for resettlement but I don't know if I am going to be resettled.'

The UN Refugee Agency, UNHCR estimates that 378,684 refugees from Syria who are in the five main host countries (Turkey, Lebanon, Jordan, Iraq and Egypt) need resettlement due to specific vulnerabilities such as serious medical needs, sexuality, gender and disability. That is why Amnesty International is calling for a global resettlement surge to relocate 380,000 Syrian refugees from the five main host countries by the end of 2016. This would amount to around 10% of the current combined Syrian refugee population in these countries being resettled to countries outside the region.

For some of these refugees, their vulnerability and need for resettlement stems from a serious medical condition or disability that cannot be treated where they are. Others face harassment, sometimes as a result of their sexuality or for being a woman without a husband.

Some have experienced extreme violence, arrest, imprisonment and torture in Syria and are unable to access the care that they need. For vulnerable refugees, being able to start their lives again in another country can have a momentous impact, giving them a lifeline and the chance of a peaceful future. However, this opportunity is dependent on wealthier countries stepping forward to open their doors and welcome Syria's refugees. This can be done via resettlement schemes, as well as by providing other forms of admission, including humanitarian admission places, family reunification, sponsorship opportunities and visas (for simplicity, these will be collectively referred to as 'resettlement').

In their own words, the refugees here describe their experiences of pre-conflict Syria, the outbreak of the crisis, their journey to neighbouring countries and their struggles as refugees. Many speak of their hopes and dreams for a safer future.

For those interviewed, a primary motivation for escape from Syria was the fear that they or their families would be harmed or killed. They witnessed random bombings, home raids, homes destroyed and people injured or killed. Beyond fearing for their own safety, parents describe wanting to protect their children from the violence and being driven by the desire to ensure their children have a good future away from the conflict.

Nadia, who has a 14-year-old son told Amnesty International, 'I heard that they kidnap children and rape women. I was very afraid. The sound of bombs made my son very afraid… I was afraid for my son so I took him and came to Jordan.'

Having made it out of Syria, refugees describe their lives in Lebanon, Jordan and Iraq, including the extreme hardships and daily struggles faced. For refugees like Qasim, his medical needs and the needs of his family have been the primary concerns. Both he and his daughter have a medical condition called elephantiasis, a disease with 'stigmatising and disabling clinical manifestations'. 'My daughter, who is 14 years-old now, has the same problem. During the last Ramadan my daughter was taken by a local NGO to a doctor and we found out she has elephantiasis. We can't afford the treatment and it is not provided in this region.' Qasim is one of over 53,000 Palestinian refugees from Syria in Lebanon who have fled Syria.

Mariam, who has three children and fled to Jordan told Amnesty International, 'In Syria you are afraid of being raped, of being arrested, of being killed and here I am afraid for my daughters. If you get sick or fall, no one is here to help you. I am struggling to buy things for my daughters.' For single parents, Yara, Nadia and Mariam, providing for their families is a continual struggle.

Women that Amnesty International spoke to face street harassment, like Yara, who describes her experiences in Lebanon: 'I wanted to register my son (aged seven) in the school. He was nagging me to be registered. While I was walking to [the place to register my son for school], some men, some with weapons surrounded and harassed me and I felt very frightened.' Other refugees, such as Hamood, have faced street harassment and abuse as a result of being gay: 'We get threats in the street every day. Sometimes we wait until it gets dark [to go out]. We are addicted to rain because the streets are empty.'

Some of the families and individuals also talk about the grinding poverty, the lack of work and the uncertainty of life as a refugee. All have hopes and dreams for the future.

However, without a significant increase in the number of resettlement places available to refugees, many vulnerable refugees will continue to face hardship. To date, the international community has done very little. In total, only 79,180 resettlement places have been offered globally by wealthier countries, a fifth of what's needed. These would only help 2.1% of the 3.8 million refugees from Syria living in Turkey, Lebanon, Jordan, Iraq and Egypt. Excluding Germany, the remaining 27 European Union countries have only offered 9,114 places, which amounts to just 0.24% of Syrian refugees in the main host countries. The six Gulf Cooperation Council (GCC) countries have offered none.

As the conflict rages on, the situation for refugees continues to deteriorate. Turkey, Lebanon, Jordan, Iraq and Egypt are between them hosting 95% of the total refugee population from Syria. To varying degrees, this has had a significant economic impact on these countries and has overstretched their infrastructure. All five of these countries have imposed restrictions on the entry of people fleeing the conflict in Syria, leaving tens of thousands, if not more, trapped in the conflict. In addition, a shortage of humanitarian funding to the region in 2014 left many refugees struggling to survive as financial aid and assistance were reduced. In December 2014, the UN launched an appeal for US$5.5 billion that will be needed in 2015 to deliver humanitarian assistance to refugees and vulnerable host communities in the region.

In this context, it is essential that the international community makes every effort to resettle far larger numbers of refugees out of the region surrounding Syria. Never has it been more pressing to call on the leaders of wealthier countries around the world to open their hearts and arms to Syria's most

vulnerable refugees and provide them with a peaceful and safe future.

Yara (23) with four children, Mahdi (7), Mariam (6), Mohamed (3), Mutanama (2)

Yara comes from Dayr al-Zor in eastern Syria and she lives alone with four young children. She told Amnesty International that her husband died in prison, which she discovered from a video on YouTube. Her two-year-old son, Mutanama, has an opening in his spine which leaks fluid into his brain. Since they moved to Lebanon in October 2012 his health has deteriorated. When she tried to register another of her children at school she was surrounded by men who harassed her. Yara and her children have moved around a lot due to unaffordable rents and the constant harassment and abuse she has faced from her family for refusing to remarry.

Yara: 'My husband was arrested by Syrian authorities at the [Lebanon/Syria] border. I didn't have anyone to turn to and people were being killed by bombings and massacres so we [her family] fled.

'I found out my husband was killed. No one told me – I found out from YouTube that my husband was detained in a [Syrian] prison. He was killed in the prison and then they threw his body outside and the rebels showed the video on YouTube. I saw the video showing his photo after he was killed. One of the sheikhs [religious leaders] told me that my husband was killed and showed me a copy of his ID card. Afterwards, the people who buried his body contacted us and told me, 'your husband is killed and come and receive his body', but we couldn't reach the place where he was. So, these same people buried him.

'I have moved around a lot in Lebanon. I can't afford to pay rent. I can't live with my parents because they have a very small house and three families already live [there]…

[My family] believe that I must get married because a woman should not stay single… they follow me to the mosque and hit me and say it's not appropriate for a woman to live all by herself… [But] my son is very sick and I [often] have to take him to hospital. The doctor [said] he mustn't be living in a crowded house or he will have diseases transferred to him.

'Mutanama [two-year-old son] has [had] an opening in his spine since [birth] and he has a device in his head. When they did the operation on his back he was only three days old. They put a device in his head because with the opening he has water [which] would go to his brain, and the device drains the water. He has a weak immune system.

'Everything is full of difficulties as a refugee; especially living here in Lebanon is very difficult. A lot of people say bad stuff about me and harass me. I used to work at a sheikh's library. I went in a taxi and told the driver I want to go to the Airport Road. He took me to Khaldi Road. He started to harass me and offered me his money and asked if I would stay with him and be his companion. I wanted to throw myself out of the car [when] we reached a checkpoint.

'I wanted to register my son [aged seven] in the school. He was nagging me to be registered. While I was walking to [the place to register her son for school], some men, some with weapons, surrounded and harassed me and I felt very frightened.

'My son's health situation is deteriorating and I would really like to treat him. The UN has put me forward for resettlement but I don't know if I am going to be resettled. I don't have anyone to help me with the children, I have no-one to support me with the rent. It's a difficult life, I can hardly manage.'

[Yara's children are asked, 'What do you like to do?']

Mariam: 'I like to play around with friends.'

Mahdi: 'I like to go to the sea. I just don't want to go back to Syria,

there's no sea [where I live] in Syria.'

Yara: They just saw the sea for the first time here. They hardly go out so they feel locked up like in prison so when they came here and saw the sea, they wanted to spend the day there.

Maher (35), Houda (30), Elias (12), Ibrahim (9), Yusra (3)

Maher, Houda and their family left Syria and have been living in Qushtapa refugee camp in the Kurdistan Region of Iraq since August 2013. Their 12-year-old son Elias was diagnosed with cancer in 2012 and they have struggled to find treatment for him amid the conflict. The hospital was shelled while Houda was inside with Elias. When Elias's hair fell out because of the cancer treatment, Maher shaved his own head too so Elias 'wouldn't know it was from the medication'. They want to be resettled so their son has access to treatment and their children can go to school.

Maher: 'We all came to Qushtapa refugee camp together. It has been a year and four months. I left because of the war and because of the lack of livelihood options. My son has cancer. He was getting treatment in Damascus. It was really hard to get the treatment because the hospital where my son was receiving treatment was in another neighbourhood. It was a troubled area so every time I used to take my son to receive treatment there were snipers and gunfire. It was very dangerous but we had to go for my son. Elias has pancreatic cancer and every three weeks we had to take him to get treatment.

'When he had his treatment, his hair fell out and I shaved my head as well so he wouldn't know it was from the medication. When we were coming back to Qamishly from Damascus, Jabhat al-Nusra [an armed group] stopped the bus and wanted to punish me because I had shaved my head and I had to explain.

Houda: 'Every time I took Elias to the hospital for his treatment I

saw a lot of fighting. There was an intense firefight with bullets hitting the hospital. I called my husband and said, 'Listen, I am really afraid'. He was outside the hospital and the doctor came and said, 'All you ladies get out of the rooms and stay in the corridors because the rooms have windows.' We started shouting and crying and we got hit by two shells. The second floor ceiling fell to the ground. All the glass broke.'

Maher: 'When I heard the shelling I ran upstairs to try to get her. One of the ceilings was open with a big hole. I did not take my son out, I did not leave. I stayed there so he could get the treatment because the doctors stayed as well. When the doctors stayed, we all stayed. It's still going on now, the bombing.

'We really hated our lives. Once we left the hospital and got the medicines [for Elias] we left. Life is very difficult here because we need doctors and medication for Elias. We have really suffered to get treatment for him. Before we left Syria he had the bone marrow test every three months and then every six months. He has been here for one year and four months and hasn't done the test. They said they weren't going to take any more x-rays and we should take him to a private hospital… For my child there is no help, no aid.

'I feel really happy we are going to be resettled to Europe because the treatment over there is much better. It [is] enough to feel like a human over there.'

Houda: 'I just want my children to be educated and I want Elias to be cured.'

4 February 2015

⇨ The above information is an extract from the Amnesty International report *Hardship, Hope and Resettlement: Refugees From Syria Tell Their Stories* and has been reprinted with permission. Please visit www.amnesty.org for further information.

I am human: refugee women's experiences of detention in the UK

We spoke to 38 women who were currently or recently detained in Yarl's Wood. 25 had been released between June 2012 and June 2014, and 13 were in detention at the time of the interview (between June and October 2014). All of these women were detained in Yarl's Wood, though three had also been detained in other places – two in Colnbrook detention centre and one in prison.

34 women disclosed the experiences in their home countries which led them to seek asylum in the UK:

⇨ 19 women said that they had been raped, 21 women had experienced other sexual violence and 24 altogether – over 70% of the 34 who answered – had experienced either rape or sexual violence. Eight had been raped by soldiers, police or prison guards.

⇨ 28 women said that they had experienced gender-related persecution under the headings we asked about – rape, sexual violence, forced marriage, forced prostitution or female genital mutilation.

⇨ 21 women said that they had been tortured, and 26 altogether said they had experienced either rape or torture.

36 women told us why they thought they had been persecuted:

⇨ 19 women, just over half, said they were persecuted because they were women.

⇨ Ten because they were politically active.

⇨ Nine because of their ethnicity.

⇨ Seven because of their religion.

⇨ Three because they were lesbians.

We asked these women if they were clear about why they were detained:

⇨ They answered in regard to 44 instances of detention (as some women had been detained more than once).

⇨ In regard to 20 instances of detention, women said that they were not clear about why they were detained.

We asked them about their experiences of being taken into detention:

⇨ Out of the 38 women, six said that they resisted detention 15, or 39%, said that they were handcuffed on detention. 13 said that between five and ten staff detained them, and one woman told us that more than ten staff were involved in detaining her. 20 said that more men than women were involved in taking them into detention, ten said it involved equal numbers of men and women.

We asked them about their experiences in Yarl's Wood:

⇨ Of 36 women who answered, 19, or more than half, were on suicide watch in Yarl's Wood.

⇨ Of 35 women who answered, 14, or 40%, said that they self-harmed in detention.

⇨ Seven out of the 38 women we spoke to were placed in Kingfisher Wing, or solitary confinement.

We asked them about how they were treated in Yarl's Wood:

⇨ Out of the 33 women who spoke about men seeing them in intimate situations, 13 said that men saw them naked, 29 said men saw them partially dressed, 29 said that men saw them in bed, 16 said men saw them in the shower and 14 said men saw them using the toilet.

⇨ Out of the 19 women who were on suicide watch, 13 said that they were watched by men, ten while they were in bed and eight while on the toilet.

⇨ Of 33 women who were watched by men, 31 said they felt uncomfortable, 29 said they felt upset, 29 felt angry, 27 felt scared and 27 were ashamed.

⇨ Out of 35 women who answered questions about being searched, 13, or a third, said that they were searched by a male member of staff. Two women said that a man searched them and asked them to take off their clothes; one of these instances was in Yarl's Wood and one in Colnbrook. 22, or two thirds, said that they experienced a man watching them while they were being searched by a female staff member.

Women also spoke about bullying, racism, and sexual suggestions and assault by staff in Yarl's Wood:

⇨ Six out of 35 said that a member of staff made a sexual suggestion to them, five of these were men.

⇨ Three of them said they were touched sexually, two by men.

⇨ Seven said they were physically assaulted, all of these by men.

⇨ 25 said that a member of staff was racist to them, 21 of these by men.

⇨ 29 of 34 said they were bullied, 24 of these by men.

Women in this sample were detained for long periods:

In our sample the shortest length of detention was two days, the longest was one year and three months, and the average length of detention was 93 days.

January 2015

⇨ The above information has been reprinted with kind permission from Women for Refugee Women. Please visit www.refugeewomen. co.uk for further information.

© *Women for Refugee Women*
2015

Raped and tortured in the Congo – left to starve in Britain

By Andrew Keefe

Marie was arrested and imprisoned for attending a peaceful anti-government demonstration organised by students at her university in the Democratic Republic of Congo. During her three months in detention she was raped, beaten and burned with cigarettes almost every day.

She arrived in the UK bearing both physical and psychological scars. Like most of the 1,000 torture survivors currently in treatment at Freedom from Torture, she displayed severe symptoms of trauma including post-traumatic stress disorder, depression and anxiety which greatly affected her daily functioning.

The sound of rattling keys and chains, doors slamming and heavy footsteps all induced flashbacks and terror for Marie. More than once the smell of cigarette smoke caused her to faint, as it was so strongly associated in her mind with her ordeal.

But when she came in for her weekly therapy sessions, Marie was often unable to talk through these deeply disturbing psychological phenomena, because she was preoccupied with far more mundane matters arising from the simple fact that she was living in dismal poverty.

In the UK most asylum seekers do not have the right to work and earn an income. They are entirely dependent on the UK Government which currently gives them just £36 per week to live on. This means that most have to make difficult decisions about essential living needs, for example whether to prioritise buying food for a nutritious meal or laundry detergent so they can wash the only set of clothes they own.

For torture survivors in particular, the impact of this additional stress can be devastating.

Research conducted by Freedom from Torture among 100 of their clients, and 18 of their frontline clinicians paints a bleak picture of financial insecurity, social exclusion and hopelessness. It confirms a disturbing reality for survivors of torture living in the UK: that their experiences of poverty compound their trauma and impede their rehabilitation.

Typically, the first phase of treatment for torture survivors involves enabling them to feel safe, secure and stable. Yet when our clients were asked about asylum support rates, the majority of those who responded said they worried 'all the time' about meeting their essential living needs. Almost all those remaining said they worried 'most' or 'some' of the time.

Poverty, and the associated insecurity, experienced by torture survivors living on asylum support in the UK reinforces symptoms of depression and post-traumatic stress disorder.

The social isolation that comes from not being able to afford to make a phone call or travel to visit family and friends, and the enforced dependency of living on asylum support, also act to reaffirm the sense of worthlessness and humiliation that is the legacy of torture on its victims.

Some of our clients also told us that a lack of funds to travel to appointments and to maintain postal or telephone contact with their therapists, GPs and other healthcare providers led to them missing appointments or even discontinuing treatment.

Another common problem our clinicians reported is that their clients are unable to participate effectively in therapy because they frequently miss meals and commonly experience hunger, poor nutrition and inadequate diet. This results in poor cognitive functioning and an inability to concentrate.

Put bluntly, it's hard to process and engage with your psychological therapy for severe trauma when you are hungry and don't know where your next meal is coming from.

On 9 April this year the High Court ruled that the Secretary of State Theresa May had used insufficient information to reach a rational decision about asylum support rates, which have remained the same for the past three years in spite of substantial increases in the cost of living. Current asylum support rates are around 50% of income support rates.

Theresa May now has until 9 August to re-assess the level at which asylum support is set in accordance with this High Court judgement. This review has the potential to lift some 20,000 of the UK's most vulnerable people, including torture survivors like Marie, out of poverty.

Both experience, and research have clearly demonstrated to those of us in the field of torture rehabilitation that levels of poverty experienced by those living on current asylum support levels actively hamper torture survivors from engaging effectively in therapy and places significant obstacles in the way of their recovery from trauma.

So as well as failing in their obligations under the Refugee Convention to offer protection to those fleeing persecution, the Home Office is currently also violating the UK's commitments under the United Nations Convention Against Torture, by which it is obliged to provide the means for the fullest rehabilitation possible to torture survivors.

Many of these concerns and findings have been echoed by myriad organisations working with asylum seekers, as well as by the

Home Affairs Select Committee in their October 2013 report. Now the High Court has ordered the Home Office to review how it sets the level of this support.

Having decided not to appeal the High Court judgement, and with the 9 August deadline for review looming, we eagerly await to see what Theresa May determines a sufficient amount to allow a dignified standard of living for asylum seekers.

And we hope it is increased to a level sufficient to allow torture survivors to engage effectively with rehabilitation and begin their recovery.

Note

Andrew Keefe is the national director of clinical services at Freedom from Torture, one of the world's largest specialist torture treatment centres. He is a psychodynamic psychotherapist and has been working with survivors of torture for the past 14 years. See www. freedomfromtorture.org for more information. Marie is a composite case study based on 34 of Freedom from Torture's female clients from the Democratic Republic of Congo. The details are all based on the typical experiences of their clients.

The opinions in politics.co.uk's Comment and Analysis section are those of the author and are no reflection of the views of the website or its owners.

4 August 2014

⇨ The above information has been reprinted with kind permission from Politics.co.uk. Please visit www.politics.co.uk for further information.

A day in the life of Joseph* in Boroli Refugee Camp, Uganda

Joseph*, a seven-year-old South Sudanese refugee, now lives with his mother and two siblings in Boroli Refugee Camp, Uganda. He is one of over 400,000 refugees who have fled South Sudan, seeking refuge from the brutal conflict that has engulfed the world's youngest nation. Over 120,000 of these are currently residing in settlement camps, like Boroli, in neighbouring Uganda. New arrivals continue to cross the border daily, often arriving exhausted, nutritionally weak and in poor health.

Joseph * attends one of Save the Children's child friendly spaces, which provides a safe environment for children to play and learn in the camp. He described his daily routine in the camp to a member of staff from Save the Children.

'It was very bad in South Sudan. We had to run because there was lots of fighting and people were being killed. I was very scared. Here it is a lot better. There is no fighting here. It is cold in the morning when we wake up, colder than it is back in South Sudan. Sometimes I don't want to get out of bed. I have to do my chores before I can go and play with my friends. First I have to dig our land so that our crops will grow. In a few months we will have our own food to eat and sell. Once I have finished digging I go and fetch water so that I can wash myself. The water is heavy but I am strong. Sometimes I practice the alphabet or my drawing outside. I use the straw from our house's roof because I don't have paper or pens. I go to the Child Friendly Space every day and it's lots of fun. We play games and swing on the swings. I like it here a lot but I want to go back to my old village in South Sudan. I love my old village.'

Currently over 350 South Sudanese children attend Save the Children's Child Friendly Space in Boroli Camp, Uganda, where they are able to play, learn and receive the support they need to move on with their lives. This is one of five child-friendly spaces run by Save the Children in refugee camps in Adjumani district in Northern Uganda.

It is estimated that, if the current trend continues, as many as 300,000 South Sudanese refugees could be sheltering in Uganda by the end of the year. Over 65% of the new arrivals are children and hundreds are arriving unaccompanied after being separated from their parents or caregivers during the fighting. In response, Save the Children is helping to register separated and unaccompanied children and then reunify them with their family members. The child-friendly spaces include Early Childhood Care and Development Centres within them, to provide refugee children in Uganda with a safe and nurturing environment in which they can play, learn and receive the support they need to move on with their lives.

* after a name indicates that the name has been changed to protect identity. This must be reflected in all usage.

⇨ The above information has been reprinted with kind permission from Save the Children. Please visit www.savethechildren.org for further information.

'Is this really Europe?': refugees in Calais speak of desperate conditions

This is an article from The Conversation.

By Thom Davies (Research Fellow at the School of Geography, Earth and Environmental Sciences at University of Birmingham), Arshad Isakjee (Research Fellow in Migration, Identity and Belonging at University of Birmingham) and Surindar Dhesi (Teaching Fellow – Environmental Health and Risk Management at University of Birmingham)

THE CONVERSATION

As the sun sets on Calais, a new barbed wire fence glints in the evening light, casting a shadow over the growing migrant camp known as the 'New Jungle'.

Through the thick undergrowth of what was once an industrial dumping ground, tents and tarpaulin structures stretch into the distance. These are the makeshift homes currently providing insufficient shelter from the elements for more than 3,000 refugees. On the other side of the fence, cars and lorries trundle towards the port of Calais – and the northern edge of the Schengen Area, where people can move freely across much of Europe.

With Operation Stack in full force, and the British Prime Minister, David Cameron, expressing 'every sympathy with holidaymakers', the body count at Calais quietly continues to rise. A migrant died on 28 July as he tried to reach the UK. He was the ninth person to lose his life to the Calais–Dover gauntlet between June and July.

Cameron has pledged that the UK Government will do everything it can to deal with this situation, but sitting in the detritus of the Calais camp, it is clear that the real crisis is humanitarian and is being fatally overlooked.

We have made two visits to Calais, spending several days at a time interviewing the camp's residents. Our research is revealing the desperate conditions in which they are living. It is time the UK and French Governments took responsibility for a shared issue. So far, all migrants are being given is more barbed wire.

Life in Calais

'When I first got to the Jungle, I thought to myself: 'is this really Europe?'' said Ilyas, a Sudanese migrant whose family were murdered by Janjaweed militia.

He showed us the rudimentary 'kitchen' he uses to cook – a dusty tent propped up with branches, with no place to safely store food. Like many, he had taken the hard route to Europe, through the Sahara desert – where three of his fellow passengers perished – and then the equally deadly boat journey across the Mediterranean.

Ilyas's friend showed us a shaky video he made on his phone of his eight-day sea crossing, this time from Egypt: 'We did not have any water for three days,' he explained, flicking through his phone to show happier images of friends and family in the country he was forced to leave.

Their troubles did not end when they reached European soil. Migrants we met in Calais who landed on Italian shores report being abandoned by authorities. Young and able men, in particular, are kept in camps for no longer than a few days; many end up homeless and hungry on the streets of Italy. As Italian agencies struggle to cope with the record numbers of migrants crossing the Mediterranean, some report being explicitly told to travel to northern European countries such as France, Germany and the UK. Others say they have even been shown a map.

So a small minority of the 137,000 migrants who have arrived in Europe so far this year have ended up in Calais. The New Jungle – less than one square kilometre in area – is where thousands of migrants live in appalling conditions that would not meet any humanitarian standards.

Toilet facilities are limited. There are two dozen portaloos and a few wooden toilet blocks with no handwashing facilities. Piles of rubbish attract rats and other pests. There is only access to cold water, often at some distance from the ad hoc living spaces. It is unsurprising then that many residents told us they are suffering from fevers, stomach pains and diarrhoea.

Some residents of the camp use chemical containers to transport water to their tents – and every morning, men, women and children as young as ten can be seen queuing for hours for a rare opportunity to gain access to a shower. At every turn, migrants can be seen limping and bedraggled, visibly injured by the increasing risks they are taking to enter the UK. Others say they are victims of police brutality and local thugs. Médecins du Monde is doing excellent work in the camp, but the scale of injury and illness is increasing.

A global crisis

Calais is undoubtedly a humanitarian and public health crisis. Yet it is only a microcosm of the migration crisis as a whole. In the world today, a population the size of Italy has been forced from their homes, putting global numbers of refugees at a level not seen since the end of World War II.

Developing countries – not European nations – host most of them. Turkey alone gives refuge to 1.7 million refugees from Syria. The next five countries hosting the largest numbers of refugees are Pakistan, Lebanon, Iran, Ethiopia and Jordan.

On the northern edge of the New Jungle, a huge bunker looms over the people queuing for a shower. Built during World War II to protect Hitler from invasion, it reminds us that this is not the first time Calais has been on the frontline of efforts to keep out perceived existential threats.

Britain's Home Secretary, Theresa May, has pledged to spend another £7 million to reinforce Fortress Calais with more barbed wire – and an archipelago of migrant camps is spreading across the continent. For her, and for the British Government, this is a security threat. Spending time with the residents of the Calais camp however, things look starkly different. It's time to wake up to the humanitarian crisis unfolding in the heart of Europe.

29 July 2015

⇨ The above information has been reprinted with kind permission from *The Conversation*. Please visit www.theconversation.com for further information.

© 2010-2015, The Conversation Trust (UK)

Still stateless, still suffering

Why Europe must act now to protect stateless persons.

Many stateless persons in Europe have claimed asylum, sometimes simply because in the absence of a statelessness determination procedure, this was the only option open to them to try and regularise their stay. In the event of asylum being refused (whether rightly or wrongly), many stateless persons are exposed to arbitrary long-term detention precisely because, lacking a nationality, they most likely cannot be removed as no other state will accept them. In some cases an individual's statelessness will only become apparent following unsuccessful efforts by a host state to re-document them during an attempted deportation process. Recent research by UNHCR has revealed the long-term detention of stateless persons to be a problem in several European countries (available at www.refworld.org/statelessness.html). The detrimental impact on stateless persons – both before, during and after detention – can be severe and is completely avoidable, as evidenced by these testimonies.

Luka

Provided by the Human Rights League, Slovakia

Luka was born in Ukraine when it was still a part of the former USSR. After growing up in an orphanage, he moved to Slovakia in 1991 when he was only 15 years old. He has never possessed any documents establishing a nationality. As a result, since becoming an adult, Luka has been repeatedly detained in Slovakia, including while police investigated the possibility of removing him to Ukraine. However, such attempts have proved fruitless because Ukraine refuses to accept him as a national. On the last occasion Luka was detained for 14 months in 2010. When ordering his release the court found that his expulsion from Slovakia was not possible and Luka was finally granted tolerated stay. However, his problems are far from over. Despite having lived in Slovakia for over 20 years, Luka is still not recognised as being stateless and his tolerated stay status does not allow him to work or to have health insurance. He cannot marry his partner or be registered officially as the father of his son. Recently, his application to renew his tolerated stay was refused due to his inability to submit new documents from the Ukrainian Embassy. He was subsequently fined for his illegal stay. This cycle shows no sign of ending.

Boban

Provided by Flemmish Refugee Action

Boban is a stateless Roma from Macedonia. Having faced discrimination his whole life – denied access to secondary school education, the right to work, the right to marry or to access social security – he decided to travel irregularly to claim asylum in Belgium in 2005. His claim was rejected so he tried to claim asylum in Luxembourg but was returned to Belgium under the Dublin Regulation. In 2008, he applied for regularisation as a stateless person, and although the process was slow his application was granted in 2009 after the Macedonian Office of Internal Affairs wrote a letter confirming that he was not a citizen of Macedonia. However, Boban was shocked to discover that his new status still gave him no right to stay in Belgium. It granted him no permission to work and no entitlement to housing or social assistance. Living destitute, his only option was again to apply for asylum. When this was refused he tried to claim asylum in Austria and Germany but on both occasions he was sent back to Belgium. On his return be claimed asylum for a sixth time and after this was rejected he was detained for three weeks even though the Belgian authorities already had confirmation from Macedonia that he was not a citizen so could not be removed there. Although now out of detention, he remains in limbo and with no hope for the future.

Roman

Provided by the Human Rights League, Slovakia

Roman was born in Kosovo in the 1960s. His father was a Yugoslav citizen and his mother was a citizen of the USSR. Early in his life, Roman's mother took him to Russia to live with his grandmother. However, before he was old enough to obtain an ID as proof of his nationality, his grandmother died and Roman left Russia to travel around Europe. He came to Slovakia more than 20 years ago but he has remained in limbo ever since due to his lack of a nationality. He describes having been held in an immigration centre on six or seven occasions due to his lack of nationality or ID. Back in 2005, he was issued with an expulsion order and a ten year re-entry ban. However, he cannot leave the country he cannot re-enter, making the ban cruelly ironic. Instead, since 2006 he has had his tolerated stay periodically extended every six months but he remains unable to get on with his life. His lack of a permanent regularised status prevents him from working or accessing other benefits which in turn impacts on his ability to care for his disabled partner, a Slovakian citizen. He cannot apply to naturalise as a Slovakian citizen because he has a criminal record due to his failure to comply with his original expulsion order (despite this being beyond his control). He has no solution in sight.

Natasha

Provided by the Human Rights League, Slovakia

Natasha was trafficked to Slovakia in 1991 and forced into prostitution. She was born and had lived her entire life in a region of the former USSR (Soviet Socialist Republic of Ukraine) which in 1991 became Moldova. Despite escaping her captors, she thereafter spent almost 20 years in Slovakia as an irregular migrant with no documents. She tried to contact the Moldovan Embassy to obtain documentation and proof of nationality but this was located in Vienna and she was not able to cross the border without a passport. Her letters to the Embassy had no effect. She applied for asylum several times but always without a result. She was detained repeatedly while the police unsuccessfully tried to deport her from Slovakia. Hardest of all, her two children – both Slovak citizens – were placed in care without her consent while she was detained. This had a devastating impact on her. Following her release from a period in detention in 2011, based on appeals submitted, the court and later the Slovak authorities recognised that her deportation was not possible while her citizenship was still undetermined. She was reunited with her children. Eventually in 2012 she was able to make use of a discretionary power enabling her to be granted permanent residence as a stateless person. After more than 22 years spent in Slovakia she was finally able to acquire all the necessary documents – a residence permit, travel document (Convention Travel Document) and health insurance card in order to get on with her life. However, Slovakia still lacks a dedicated statelessness determination procedure to protect all stateless migrants in this situation and to prevent their arbitrary detention.

Rashid

Provided by the Tilburg University Statelessness Programme

Rashid was born in Myanmar. He fled to Bangladesh aged 12 with his mother in 1992 after his father, who was a Muslim rights activist, was killed and his sister was arrested. He lived in Bangladesh for 20 years, first in a refugee camp and then in several villages. Before Rashid's mother passed away in 2002 she explained to Rashid that he did not possess a valid identity document because the Rohingya of Myanmar had been deprived of their Myanmar nationality. Rashid travelled irregularly to The Netherlands in 2012. He applied for asylum twice and his request was refused both times. After the second rejection he was kept in immigration detention for eight months. He was eventually released after being presented to the Bangladeshi and Myanmar authorities, both of which refused to accept him as a national. However, following his release he was unable to regularise his stay and he remains without status and sleeps in a homeless shelter. He has lived with instability his entire life and now finds himself alone in a foreign country suffering from nightmares, psychological issues and high blood pressure (even though he is still a young man). He cannot lead a normal life in The Netherlands but equally he cannot go and live anywhere else.

2014

⇨ The above information is from the European Network on Statelessness report *Still Stateless. Still Suffering* (http://www.statelessness.eu/sites/www.statelessness.eu/files/ENS_Still_Stateless_Still_Suffering_online%20version_2.pdf) and has been reprinted with kind permission from the European Network on Statelessness. Please visit www.statelessness.eu for further information.

© European Network on Statelessness 2014

Detention centres in the UK: a question of double standards

It has been reported on many occasions that some immigrants wait up to five years in detention for their cases to be resolved. But this time a report reveals the accounts of 26 witnesses, together with 182 written declarations, figures for absurd detentions and abuses on the part of the authorities.

By Virginia Moreno Molina

Abdal, a man now aged 30, came to the United Kingdom in 2003 and sought asylum after being tortured and persecuted in Sudan because of his political activity.

He has over 200 scars on his body, although he does not like to talk about his experience.

'As one of the longest-serving detainees in UK history, he was detained altogether for over five years and was transferred to nearly every single detention centre across the UK. His experiences of detention served to both exacerbate existing trauma but also created new mental health issues. Since his release from detention, he is on 17 different kinds of medication.'

Abdal's case forms part of the investigation: The *Report of the Inquiry into the use of Immigration Detention in the United Kingdom*. It demonstrates the ineffectiveness of detention, as well as the way people are treated when they are arrested and sent to detention centres, which seems to approach and even cross the boundary of illegality.

This is because, instead of seeking ways to improve their lives and make them more comfortable, the number of detainees continues to rise. At the end of September 2014, 3,378 people were in detention, many of them waiting months or years for their cases to be resolved.

The figures showed a 24% increase on 2013, an alarming figure, but despite this a new expansion of the Campsfield Detention Centre is planned.

The issue has returned to the attention of the media in the run-up to the May General Elections. And this is due to the intention of the Inquiry members, that the report should serve as a guide for the new Government to set up a group of specialists to deal with the problem and take the necessary measures.

The investigation was put in motion and carried out by the All Party Parliamentary Group on Refugees and the All-Party Parliamentary Group on Migration, which are made up of MPs and Members of the House of Lords. They are unofficial groups unlike Select Committees, so their work carries less weight.

Both groups met in July 2014 to discuss the issues around the situation and to propose solutions. Later they held three hearings during which 26 witnesses recounted their experiences, and 182 written statements were considered.

Unlimited detention

Sarah, one of the witnesses heard during the Inquiry put it like this: 'The lack of time limit is the worst part of it, as you don't know when or if you will get out. You can't say to yourself 'tomorrow I'll be OK'. Tomorrow you will be locked in or flown back to the country where you are afraid for your life.'

This is because the UK is one of the few countries of the Council of Europe in which there is no limit on the time a person can be detained. It is not unusual for someone to spend up to four years or even more in one of these centres, without knowing what their fate will be. And although EU Returns Directive 2008/115/EC exists, which introduced a six month limit on detentions – which can be extended to 12 months if the detainee refuses to cooperate in the process – the UK does not apply this Directive.

In reply to a Parliamentary Question on this subject in 2010 to the Minister of State for Borders and Immigration, Labour MP Phil Woolas, he replied that: 'Our current practices on the return of illegal third country nationals are broadly in line with the terms of the Directive, but we prefer to formulate our own policy...'

The members of the All-Party Group are proposing a maximum detention period of 28 days, which should also only be used as a last resort because, in addition to the revelation of the psychological impact that detentions have, their monetary cost is disproportionate. For the year 2013/14 the cost of detention was £164.4 million, equivalent to £36,026 for each person detained per year.

Shortcomings and abuses

Since September 2014 the NHS has been responsible for health services in Detention Centres.

But prior to this there had been many complaints of abuse and poor treatment.

One among many happened in 2011, when a woman called Sana contacted *The Observer* newspaper to say that while she was in Yarl's Wood, she complained of a headache to one of the nurses, who told her that 'she did not need medication but needed his penis'.

And the situation has not improved. A recent investigation by Channel 4 revealed that employees in Yarl's Wood described detainees as 'animals' or 'foxes'. Also, according to the report, medical consultations last only ten minutes, without professionals qualified to deal with the basics, and in the presence of guards, which women complained about.

In addition, Dr Danny Allen, a psychiatrist with experience in Detention Centres, stated in the investigation that detainees are asked on arrival for consent to make their medical records available to the Home Office. But the possible use of the records in assessing whether a detainee can remain in the UK is 'alarming' according to the report.

The Group recommends that there should always be the opportunity to speak in confidence during a consultation; that these should be at least 30 minutes; and that no requests for medical records should be made on their arrival.

Rule 35

According to the report, 'Rule 35 of the Detention Centre Rules mandates that detention centre doctors must inform the Home Office of a potential victim of torture for a review to be carried out.'

The report also gives examples of a number of situations experienced in these places: 'One client who disclosed a history of multiple-perpetrator rape by a violent gang was told that her situation did not warrant a Rule 35 report. In the medical notes, the doctor concludes: 'rape – private. No Rule 35…'.

Another victim who reported being the victim of an 'honour crime', was told to 'go and google 'torture' – presumably a reference to the fact that as the ill treatment did not come at the hands of state actors it did not qualify as torture.'

But according to the figures, in the second four-month period of 2014, 452 detainees were the subjects of investigations under Rule 35, and only 45 were freed as a result.

Women: an easy target

'72% of the women who have spoken about their experiences as detainees had been raped and persecuted in their countries', according to Women for Refugee Women.

They fled from their homes, only to find themselves in a situation similar to the one they were trying to escape from. This is what has been shown, since Yarl's Wood has been the cause of several scandals related to indignities and abuses on the part of personnel.

In January 2015, Women for Refugee Women published a report in which it revealed that: 'In June 2014 the management of Yarl's Wood said that 31 allegations of sexual contact had been investigated and ten staff had been dismissed. Six women in our sample said that staff at Yarl's Wood had made sexual suggestions to them, and three said that they were touched sexually.'

Besides this the investigating group said that they made known that:

'pregnant women had been obliged to travel long distances, sometimes for several days'.

The report recommends that people who may have suffered torture, rape, trafficking, or are pregnant not be detained due to the risk of causing them further trauma.

Double standards

However, although the current anti-immigrant policy, states the 'intention' to reduce immigration to the UK, the real situation seems to be very different, if the history of detention centres is examined.

In the last two decades, the expansion of these places has been very rapid, with figures changing across the years. In 1993 there were 250 places available: 2,665 at the beginning of 2009, and 3,915 at the start of 2015.

And recently the District of Cherwell has been considering expanding the capacity of Campsfield from 276 to 600 places.

In addition, in the case that insufficient places are available, the Home Office and the National Offender Management Service will have the power, under an agreement, to place people in prisons, according to comments in the investigation.

It is also important to recall that, 'companies like Serco, GEO Group, G4S or Mitie have detainees working in detention centres for £1 or £1.25 an hour, six times less than the minimum wage'.

This was exposed in the investigation *True Scale of Captive Migrant Labour Revealed*, undertaken by Phil Miller, who spoke to The Prisma on the subject.

(Translated by Graham Douglas.)

29 March 2015

⇨ The above information is reprinted with kind permission from *The Prisma – The Multicultural Newspaper.* Please visit www.theprisma. co.uk for further information.

New report reveals stigma and hunger for asylum seekers who have to live without cash

A new report by the British Red Cross exposes the failings of the Azure payment card – and calls for asylum seekers to receive this support in cash.

'The Azure payment card' report uses questionnaires and in-depth interviews to explore how well the card works – from the viewpoint of asylum seekers and the organisations that support them.

A cashless system

The Azure card is given to refused asylum seekers who are destitute and cannot return home, for reasons beyond their control. They can legally stay in the UK, but are not allowed to work.

The Government gives them temporary accommodation, on a no-choice basis, and the Azure card. The card is pre-loaded with £35.39 a week for single asylum seekers.

Skipped meals

The report finds that those who live off the card often struggle to meet their basic needs. Some interviewees we spoke to said they were unable to eat three meals a day.

This is sometimes due to failures and restrictions with the system, which can leave people without financial support for days.

Using the card can also cause stigma and embarrassment at the checkout.

One interviewee told us: 'It's a kind of jail... and your dignity is literally taken away from you because of a simple card.'

Cash, not cards

Jonathan Ellis, head of policy, research and advocacy at the Red Cross, said: 'With strong support from Red Cross offices and our partners across the UK, we feel that we have produced a compelling report which calls for the abolition of the Azure payment card.

'This card is causing a humanitarian crisis among some asylum seekers. It is time for change.

'We urge the Government to scrap this restrictive card that causes so much unnecessary suffering and re-introduce cash support.'

25 July 2014

⇨ The above information is reprinted with kind permission from the British Red Cross. Please visit www.redcross.org.uk for further information.

Risking death in the Mediterranean: the least bad option for so many migrants

Inmates of a Libyan migrant detention centre explain why the often lethal gamble of sea crossings hold no fear when escaping tyranny, hunger and disease.

By Patrick Kingsley

Sobbing and shaking, Mohamed Abdallah tries to explain why he still wants to risk crossing the Mediterranean Sea in an inflatable boat. He sits in a migrant detention centre in Zawya, Libya, surrounded by hundreds of fellow asylum seekers who nearly died this week at sea.

They survived only after being intercepted, detained and brought back to shore by Libyan coastguards, ending a week in which they went round in circles, starving and utterly lost. But despite their horror stories, Abdallah, 21, says the journey that his fellow inmates barely withstood – and that killed more than 450 others this week – is his only option.

'I cannot go back to my country,' says Abdallah, who is from Darfur, in Sudan. He left for what is now South Sudan in 2006, after he says his village was destroyed in the Darfur war, his father died, and his sisters raped. But in South Sudan, another war later broke out. So he made his way through the Sahara, a journey that he says killed his brother and cousin, to Libya. And there last year, he was witness to his third civil war in a decade – a war that still drags on, its frontline just a few miles from the camp at Zawya.

'There is a war in my country, there's no security, no equality, no freedom,' Abdallah says. 'But if I stay here, it's just like my country. There is no security, there is violence. When you work, they take your money.'

He worked in a soap shop, and saved up to pay local smugglers for the boat to Europe. But just as he hoped to complete the payment, he was robbed, and then arrested. The recounting of his ordeal brings out first the tears, and then a conclusion: 'I need to go to Europe.'

Shuffling shoeless around the sandy courtyard, queuing for their daily bowl of rice and a potato, there are 350 men and women who very recently wanted the same. There are Eritreans here, fleeing one of the world's harshest dictatorships. There are Ghanaians – often migrants in search of jobs. There are people escaping conflict in Nigeria, Chad and Ivory Coast. And a man from Sierra Leone, Abu Bakr, who says both his parents died in last year's ebola outbreak.

Around 120 had been at sea for a week, drifting aimlessly. Libyan smugglers had crammed them on the boat with just a compass and no driver. 'No one knew where we were going,' says Vincent Collins, a 24-year-old Nigerian who arrived here a day ago. His pregnant wife Jennifer is locked in a separate cell. 'Everyone had an idea, everyone was trying to drive the boat,' Collins adds. 'We were just following the sun.'

The bread and water – just three-dozen 500ml bottles – ran out after two days. With nowhere to move, men in the middle of the boat simply urinated onto their neighbours. 'They pissed on all our clothes,' says Fatima Bahgar, a 20-year-old Malian student. 'I was sick of the scent.' At the edge of the boat, two men overbalanced, fell into the water, and drowned. A third seemed to be overwhelmed by the situation, or the thirst, and tried to sabotage the boat himself. 'So the other boys,' says Bahgar, 'put him over the side...'

Record numbers of migrants are dying in the Mediterranean this year, amid the largest wave of mass-migration since the Second World War. So far in 2015, nearly 1,000 asylum seekers have drowned, including 450 this week in at least three separate incidents. That puts the death toll at around 20 times higher than the equivalent figure in 2014, which was itself a record year.

Last October, EU officials hoped to curb the death rate by scaling back full-scale Italian-run search-and-rescue missions, arguing they were simply encouraging more people to come. Operation Mare Nostrum saved around 100,000 lives last year, but politicians said they felt they could save more by ending it.

This year's events suggest otherwise. Deaths have increased exponentially, but have failed to deter others risking the same fate. The number of those attempting the journey from the Libyan coast – and to a lesser extent from Egypt – has remained at the same high level. The explanation from migrant after migrant at Zawya is simple. The risk of death at sea is no worse than the dire circumstances they found themselves either in their home country, or in Libya.

Eritreans formed the second largest group of immigrants to Europe last year, after Syrians, and at Zawya they are among the most vocal. An Eritrean nurse, Bayin Keflemekal, describes the horror of home, where anyone suspected of breathing a word of dissent is imprisoned, and where emigration is all but banned. 'Our country is a total dictatorship,' says Keflemekal, 30. 'They can put us in prison for unlimited years. If we go back we will die.'

Conditions in the nearby countries of northern and eastern Africa are hardly more secure. Time and again, neighbouring governments have not upheld their obligations to refugees – with Egypt and Sudan among the states that have in recent years deported Eritreans back to their military regime. In Libya, their precarious position has been compounded by the war, which has forced the world's two largest refugee advocates – the UN refugee agency (UNHCR), and the International Organization for Migration (IOM) – to drastically reduce their operations.

'It is not our choice to penetrate the sea,' says Keflemekal. 'If we got some help from the Libyan Government, from UNHCR, we would try something else. But if the Government won't help us, if UNHCR won't help us, if no one can help us, then the only option is to go to the smugglers. We are suspended in the air.'

Not everyone has such heart rending reasons for risking the Mediterranean. One woman wants to get to Europe because she believes she is more likely to get a visa to visit her brother in America. A Ghanaian says he isn't fleeing political persecution but just wants a job. But almost all have ended up in a situation that forces them to go to sea.

Some may have come to Libya as a destination in itself, looking for work. But often their employers take their passports, and essentially treat them as slave labour. If they protest, they risk being reported to the police. And if they leave

entirely, they risk being arrested as an illegal migrant.

'If they escape, they have no other options,' says Zakariya el-Zaidi, the co-founder of Mercy Wings, a NGO in Tripoli that combats human trafficking. 'They can't reach out to their embassy because they have no other identification. And some of them really can't go back to their countries, and they can't claim asylum here. Libya doesn't really recognise asylum seekers.'

The situation at Zawya, nominally one of the better detention centres in Libya, typifies that country's approach. The camp's guards speak with some compassion and sincerity about the inmates. In the absence of central funding, they say they pay for the inmates' daily rice from their own pocket, and want foreign help to set up a proper blood-test centre.

But the conditions are harsh; the rooms reek of urine and they squeeze more than 60 detainees into each. There are no beds. The inmates complain of beatings, though the camp commander says this is 'just occasional' and 'essential crowd control'.

The inmates' frustration is understandable: many of them are

detained for months on end, without any hope of release. The camp commander, Colonel Khaled Tomy, admits this is a problem. But says his hands are tied by the war, which has left Libya ruled by two parallel governments. 'Ideally they wouldn't stay more than a month,' says Tomy. 'But the problem is that processing isn't happening. Diplomats aren't in Libya at the moment, and we don't have buses or vans to transport them.'

But some people do get released. Tomy says local militias have occasionally come to take the most battle-ready migrants to fight in the civil war. Other inmates report that you can leave for a bribe. 'Why are we asked to pay 1,000 dinars [around £250] to leave?' asks one. 'Why?'

If and when they do leave, some inmates claim they'll go straight back home, and won't risk the sea again. But the guards say this is just talk: they see the same faces return again and again. Even with the rise in deaths, the lure of Europe is too great.

Late at night, back in the suburbs of Tripoli, a Ghanaian called Abdo underlines why. His friends all know about the deaths at sea this week, he says. But they'll risk the journey anyway because, once again, they feel it's the least worst option. 'We follow the news on the African TV and the BBC, we know what's going on,' says the 32-year-old

'We call each other, we say, "eh, man, you see what's happening?" But you know in French we say: "Cabri mort n'a pas peur du couteau" … A dead goat doesn't fear the butcher's knife.'

17 April 2015

⇨ The above information is reprinted with kind permission from *The Guardian*. Please visit www.theguardian.com for further information.

Disabled refugees must not be forgotten

Today (20 June 2014), on World Refugee Day, Handicap International is voicing serious concerns about the situation facing disabled and vulnerable refugees worldwide.

According to the UN, the number of people forced to flee their homes because of war or persecution exceeded 50 million in 2013, the first time since World War Two. The overall figure is six million higher than the year before, an increase fuelled by conflicts in Central Africa, South Sudan and Syria.

Over 2.8 million people have now fled the fighting in Syria and sought refuge in neighbouring countries. Lebanon has already taken in almost one third of the total number of Syrian refugees, over one million people in the last three years. Despite the best efforts of humanitarian organisations, including Handicap International, the refugees' living conditions remain appalling. Handicap International denounces the risks the most vulnerable populations are exposed to and the threat to a country which is struggling to cope with the enormous impact of increasing numbers of refugees.

Today, Lebanon, the first of Syria's neighbours to have opened its borders to those fleeing the fighting, faces a major challenge as it tries to absorb one million refugees. In the last three years, Lebanon's population has gone from four to five million people. In some areas of the country, notably along the Syrian border, the local population is made up of more Syrians than Lebanese. For instance, the town of Arsal had 40,000 inhabitants before the war. It is now home to 100,000 people.

The situation for Syrian refugees is becoming increasingly precarious as the possibilities for hosting new arrivals decrease. The demographic and humanitarian consequences of this sudden overpopulation are disastrous.

According to a report launched in April by Handicap International and HelpAge International, 20% of refugees in Lebanon have a physical, mental or sensory impairment and over 30% of refugees have some form of vulnerability (injury, disability, chronic disease, etc.) resulting from their situation.

'Our teams working in Lebanon are finding that the Syrian families are exhausted, some of them have been in the country for several years and their resources have run out,' explains Aleema Shivji, Director of Handicap International UK. The overpopulation is also bringing financial hardship on vulnerable Lebanese families. According to the International Labour Organization, around 170,000 Lebanese people have fallen below the poverty line, joining the one million people already living in precarious circumstances.

'We are constantly reviewing our set-up by regularly putting into place new projects and adapting our operational approaches' explains Ms Shivji. 'In practice, over the last few months, we have reinforced our system for the reception of new refugees arriving from Syria. We are on hand, even during the night if required, to identify the most vulnerable people and people with disabilities.'

Since the start of the crisis, Handicap International's 450-strong team has helped over 180,000 people. In Syria, we meet the post-operative needs of injured people in several health centres. We also identify disabled and injured people in camps and communities, provide them with follow-up rehabilitation care, and hand out food baskets and hygiene kits. In Lebanon and Jordan, Handicap International's response focuses on identifying and supporting the most vulnerable people and providing physical rehabilitation services to people with injuries and disabilities. We also supply essential non-food items to new arrivals living in conditions of extreme hardship, along with financial assistance to families in distress, and psychosocial support.

20 June 2014

⇨ The above information is reprinted with kind permission from Handicap International. Please visit www.handicap-international.org.uk for further information.

Calais crisis: UN official slams the UK Government for accepting fewer refugees than neighbours

By Cahal Milmo

A senior United Nations official has sharply criticised the British response to the crisis in Calais, saying that the UK accepts far fewer refugees than its neighbours and any threat posed by migrants had been 'exaggerated beyond belief'.

Peter Sutherland, the UN special representative on migration, called for a change in policy as Prime Minister David Cameron was condemned by welfare groups and his opponents for describing migrants arriving across the Mediterranean as a 'swarm'.

The Channel Tunnel freight terminal was once more targeted on Wednesday night by groups of refugees trying to board trains bound for Britain. The incursions were the third night running that significant numbers had entered the site, often with fatal consequences after a young Sudanese man was killed on Tuesday – the latest of nine deaths since June.

Humanitarian groups questioned figures claiming that up to 3,000 people have 'stormed' the Tunnel this week, saying that the official tally in fact represents multiple attempts by the same individuals and the numbers disrupting the site were not exceeding 500. In Kent, some 6,000 lorries last night remained in Operation Stack, awaiting passage to France after days of disruption.

Mr Sutherland said that claims in some quarters of the British media that the UK is facing an invasion of asylum seekers from Calais were calculated to 'inflame tensions' over the issue.

He told Ireland's RTE Radio: 'The fact remains last year the total approval in France of refugees was 68,000 – that is more than twice the figure of the UK.

'I find it quite amazing the accounts that are being given in the UK media in regard to Calais. Suggesting the UK is being flooded with asylum seekers and that this creates a real threat is absolute nonsense.'

Highlighting the living conditions of the estimated 4,000 migrants in Calais, most of them crowded into a semi-official shanty town known as the 'new jungle', Mr Sutherland added that the Government was 'being very careful to ensure they do not come to Britain'.

Mr Cameron had earlier vowed that Britain would not be a 'safe haven' for illegal migrants and warned those without valid grounds for asylum would be removed. Speaking in Vietnam, the Prime Minister added: 'This is very testing, I accept that, because you have got a swarm of people coming across the Mediterranean, seeking a better life, wanting to come to Britain because Britain has got jobs, it's got a growing economy, it's an incredible place to live.'

Downing Street insisted Mr Cameron had been trying to emphasise the 'scale' of migrant numbers entering Europe. But human rights groups condemned the Conservative leader's choice of language. Lisa Doyle, head of advocacy for the Refugee Council, said: 'It's extremely disappointing to hear the Prime Minister using such irresponsible, dehumanising language to describe the desperate men, women and children fleeing for their lives across the Mediterranean Sea.

'This sort of rhetoric is extremely inflammatory and comes at a time when the Government should be focused on working with its European counterparts to respond calmly and compassionately to this dreadful humanitarian crisis.'

Liberal Democrat leader Tim Farron said Mr Cameron was running the risk of 'dehumanising some of the world's most desperate people'. He added: 'We are talking about human beings here, not insects. By using the Prime Minister's language we lost sight of how desperate someone has to be to cling to the bottom of a lorry or train for the chance of a better life.'

A medical charity meanwhile warned of dire health problems being faced by migrants in the 'new jungle' and called for a proportion of the funds being provided by Britain to secure transport hubs in Calais to be spent on humanitarian aid.

Leigh Daynes, executive director of Doctors of the World UK, which has staff working in Calais, said: 'These are ordinary people – mothers, fathers, daughters and sons – living in the most horrendous conditions that no one should have to endure.

'Many are highly educated, including doctors, dentists and engineers, fleeing extreme violence and poverty and simply wanting better lives for themselves, so much so they are prepared to risk their lives for it.'

The effects of the migrant arrivals and associated disruption also continued to be felt in Britain. Kent County Council said it was struggling to cope with a surge in the number of minors claiming asylum after arriving unaccompanied in Dover and Folkestone.

The local authority said the number of migrants aged under 18 in its care had almost doubled to 605 in the last three months and it had approached the Home Office for additional support.

In the meantime, organisers of the UK's most prestigious outdoor showjumping event said a suspected Sudanese migrant had been found hidden under a horsebox.

Staff at the All England Jumping Course in Hickstead, West Sussex, said the 26-year-old man had been discovered on Tuesday beneath a Belgian-registered lorry. After being checked by medical personnel he was passed to Sussex Police.

30 July 2015

⇨ Information from *The Independent*. Please visit www.independent.co.uk for further information.

World leaders accused of shameful failure over refugee crisis

Scathing Amnesty report says leaders guilty of neglect as millions face misery in 'worst refugee crisis of our era'.

By Kareen Shaheen

Millions of refugees have been condemned to a life of misery in the worst displacement crisis since the Second World War, a leading human rights organisation has said in a scathing report that blames world leaders' neglect for the deaths of thousands of civilians fleeing wars in the Middle East and Africa.

'We are witnessing the worst refugee crisis of our era, with millions of women, men and children struggling to survive amidst brutal wars, networks of people traffickers and governments who pursue selfish political interests instead of showing basic human compassion,' said Salil Shetty, Amnesty International's Secretary General, in a statement.

'The refugee crisis is one of the defining challenges of the 21st century, but the response of the international community has been a shameful failure.'

The report, titled *The Global Refugee Crisis: A Conspiracy of Neglect*, places a particular focus on the Syrian crisis.

Almost four million people displaced from Syria have registered with the UN High Commissioner for refugees. The burden has fallen almost entirely on the shoulders of neighbouring states, who host 95% of the refugees. In Lebanon, one in five people is a Syrian refugee, the equivalent per capita of the UK hosting nearly 13 million refugees.

With its infrastructure stretched beyond breaking point and its government in a state of disarray, Lebanon has imposed a series of restrictions on the entry of refugees that has led to an 80% drop in new registrations compared with last year, despite the continued ferocity of the Syrian civil war.

The report concluded that the countries hosting Syrian refugees have received 'almost no meaningful international support', with the UN's humanitarian appeal to cover the costs of caring for the refugees receiving less than a quarter of the necessary funds. In Turkey, border guards used water cannon over the weekend to push back a fresh influx of refugees fleeing the fighting between Islamic State militants and Kurdish militias near the long border with Syria.

Amnesty criticised the international community for similarly failing to respond to massive displacement crises in sub-Saharan Africa, where there are an estimated three million refugees, including hundreds of thousands who have fled conflicts in Nigeria, South Sudan, the Central African Republic and Burundi in recent years.

On the Mediterranean migrant crisis, Amnesty called on European nations to share the burden of resettling refugees, and said the scaling back of Operation Mare Nostrum – the Italian effort to handle asylum seekers fleeing to Europe by boat – had contributed to the increase in the number of people drowning.

About 3,500 people died while trying to cross the Mediterranean to Europe in 2014, with 1,865 dying this year so far. The majority of those fleeing by boat are Syrians displaced by the war.

'The European governments have pushed them back into the sea rather than resettle them,' Shetty said at the report's launch in Beirut. More generally, Shetty added, the world is 'turning its back to the most vulnerable people'.

In south-east Asia, 300 refugees and migrants have died at sea due to starvation, dehydration and abuse by boat crews, with Indonesia, Malaysia and Thailand initially refusing to allow boats carrying migrants to land back, putting many at risk. Amnesty castigated the Australian Government in particular for 'harsh, humiliating' conditions in which asylum seekers are kept when they attempt to reach the country.

Amnesty estimated the number of displaced people globally to be above 50 million, a crisis greater in magnitude than any since the Second World War.

The rights group called on states to resettle 1.5 million refugees over the next five years, prioritise saving the lives of displaced people over domestic immigration policies, create a refugee fund, hold a global summit to deal with the crisis, and ratify the UN's refugee convention.

15 June 2015

⇨ The above information is reprinted with kind permission from *The Guardian*. Please visit www.theguardian.com for further information.

Refugees have no safe way to reach Britain, but we can provide it

By Sonya Sceats

As is blindingly obvious, there are high numbers of refugees aboard the dilapidated boats making their way cross the Mediterranean. According to figures from UNHCR and Frontex, the EU agency that coordinates border control, most passengers are fleeing conflict-afflicted or fragile states.

One in three is Syrian. Another third come from Afghanistan, Eritrea, Somalia and Nigeria. All of these countries have abysmal human rights records, as Freedom from Torture knows well from the torture survivors to whom we provide therapeutic and other clinical services.

We also know that torture survivors are risking their lives on the boats because we work with and alongside many who have only reached us after braving this perilous crossing. They tell of appalling mistreatment, over-crowding and dehydration, and shared fears among all those on board that they will drown at sea.

We welcome the Prime Minister's remark in Parliament that 'when people are fleeing torture and persecution, they can find a home here in Britain'. The big problem is that they lack safe and legal means of getting here.

Torture survivors cannot apply for asylum at British embassies. Realistically, the only way is to turn up at the border by any means possible.

A better way is for the UK to agree safe passage in advance for torture survivors and other vulnerable refugees identified by the UN High Commissioner for Refugees in refugee camps and elsewhere, often in countries bordering conflict zones.

The UK makes a paltry contribution to such programmes. In the last year we offered a new start to only 934 refugees identified by the UNHCR as needing sanctuary. A special scheme for Syrians, created in response to enormous public pressure, has only helped 187 people.

Germany has offered to resettle 20,000 Syrian refugees and Canada has pledged to take 10,000. Compared with the UK's programmes for Syrians and refugees from other parts of the world, Sweden and Norway both offer twice as many places.

From across the political spectrum, including within the Conservative movement, calls are rising for the UK to take more.

While the Prime Minister has made clear his opposition to the EU's plans to set mandatory resettlement quotas, he has not ruled out a voluntary pledge.

As a collective European problem, the Mediterranean crisis is high on the agenda of a meeting of EU home affairs ministers on Tuesday and it will also be debated at an EU summit on 25 June which the Prime Minister himself will attend.

Ahead of these discussions, he has an opportunity to shift the focus from what his government will not do, to show instead what it will do.

By announcing a significant increase in resettlement opportunities, David Cameron would give meaning to his assertion that 'Britain is a country with a moral conscience – we do not walk on by'.

Such a move would reassure the public that Britain's immigration policies are underpinned by fairness and compassion where this is undeniably called for.

It would make good on the Conservative Party's manifesto promise to continue British leadership in helping vulnerable women and children fleeing violence in Syria and, we would hope, other war-torn states.

And it would allow the Prime Minister to lead by example after his earlier calls for European states to cooperate in finding solutions to this humanitarian crisis.

Of course any pledge to resettle more refugees must be part of a multi-pronged approach, spanning measures to prevent torture and other root causes of flight, regional aid to states bearing the brunt of displacement and a fair asylum system for those who make it here, including early identification of torture survivors and proper handling of medical evidence.

Responding to the outpouring of public sympathy after the mass drownings in April the Prime Minister conceded that 'Britain can do more to lend a hand'. His decision to resume participation in search and rescue operations and the heroic work of HMS Bulwark is a welcome start. There is room to be much more generous on refugee resettlement and the time to act is now.

Sonya Sceats is director of policy and advocacy at Freedom from Torture. Follow her at @SonyaSceats.

15 June 2015

⇨ The above information is reprinted with kind permission from Politics.co.uk. Please visit their website for further information.

To deal with the refugee crisis you need to understand the cause

***An article from The* Conversation.**

By Alexander Betts, Leopold Muller Associate Professor in Refugee and Forced Migration Studies at University of Oxford

THE CONVERSATION

The ongoing crisis in the Mediterranean, which has seen more than 30 times as many people die as in the same period last year, has evoked unprecedented media attention. What should be about a humanitarian tragedy has become hijacked by opportunist politicians, who in many cases have fundamentally and wilfully misrepresented the underlying causes of the problem. If solutions are based on that misrepresentation, they will fail and have harmful consequences.

From early in the week, Italy's Prime Minister, Matteo Renzi, focused on proclaiming a 'war on trafficking', describing it as 'the slavery of our time'.

UK Foreign Secretary, Phillip Hammond and others followed suit. Yet there are at least two problems with this narrative. First, it fails to distinguish between 'trafficking' and 'smuggling', the former being irrelevant in this context.

Second, and more importantly, it fails to recognise that smuggling does not cause migration, it responds to an underlying demand. Criminalising the smugglers serves as a convenient scapegoat. But it cannot solve the problem. It will simply displace the problem, increase prices, introduce ever less scrupulous market entrants, and make journey ever more perilous.

Crisis of displacement

The real causes of the tragedy are two-fold. First, we need to situate the tragedy in a broader context. There is a global displacement crisis. Around the world, more people are displaced than at any time since the Second World War. Globally, there are more than 50m displaced

and 16 million refugees. To take the case of Syria, there are nine million displaced Syrians; three million of whom are refugees. Most are in Turkey, Jordan, and Lebanon. But countries like Jordan and Lebanon – whose capacities are stretched to breaking point – are now closing their borders and in need of international burden-sharing. These people have to go somewhere and increasingly they are travelling on to Europe in search of protection.

Second, the cause of the deaths can be directly linked to Europe's decision to end the Italian search and rescue operation Mare Nostrum in November 2014 and replace it with the inadequately funded EU-run Operation Triton. Mare Nostrum saved more than 100,000 lives last year. Since the ending of Mare Nostrum, many fewer have been rescued and many more have died. To address the crisis, it is these two

causes that need to be looked at first.

We know from existing data that the people crossing the Mediterranean are increasingly from refugee-producing countries such as Syria, Eritrea and Somalia. While some – coming from West Africa – may well be more likely to be leaving poverty or seeking opportunity, a huge proportion are therefore fleeing conflict and persecution and are in need of international protection.

We have international legal obligations to protect such people. Yet the EU has largely failed to recognise this. On Monday, the EU held an emergency meeting in Luxembourg at which it produced a ten-point plan. This was vague in detail but the emphasis was on dismantling the smugglers and on containing migration from within North Africa. References to humanitarian roles

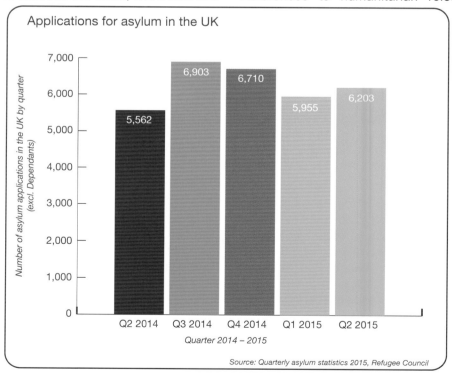

Applications for asylum in the UK

Number of asylum applications in the UK by quarter (excl. Dependants)

- Q2 2014: 5,562
- Q3 2014: 6,903
- Q4 2014: 6,710
- Q1 2015: 5,955
- Q2 2015: 6,203

Quarter 2014 – 2015

Source: Quarterly asylum statistics 2015, Refugee Council

such as expanding Triton and refugee resettlement remained under-specified. The logic, in other words, was primarily about containment and counter-smuggling operations.

This emphasis has been repeated in the leaked draft statement of the EU Summit. The statement highlights deportation and immigration control; it is a manifesto for containment. It proposes to deport 150,000 people and offer relocation across Europe of up to a quota of 5,000 while emphasising the aspiration to bolster Libya's capacity to control migration to the EU. It again shows a misunderstanding of the underlying causes of the problem, and it is likely to be inconsistent with international refugee and human rights law.

There are no simple solutions to this issue. But the key to finding solutions is by putting the issue in its broader context. The UN rapporteur on the human rights of migrants, Francois Crepeau, has been among the most articulate in highlighting this.

A joint statement by Antonio Guterres, Peter Sutherland, Bill Swing and Zeid Ra'ad Al Hussein has emphasised the need for solutions that go beyond the 'minimalist' EU response. These include a well-resourced search-and-rescue operation; channels for safe and regular migration; making a firm commitment to receive significantly higher numbers of refugees through EU-wide resettlement; bolstering arrangements for more equitable burden-sharing within Europe and combating racism and xenophobia. These are sensible solutions and advance the debate.

However, to ultimately, address the underlying causes of the issue, a global and comprehensive approach is needed. It is a symptom of a global displacement crisis, needs to be addressed in a comprehensive way.

Learning from history

There are instructive lessons from history. After the end of the Vietnam War in 1975, literally hundreds of thousands of Indochinese 'boat people' crossed territorial waters from Vietnam, Laos and Cambodia towards South-East Asian host states such as Malaysia, Singapore, Thailand, the Philippines, as well as Hong Kong. Throughout the 1970s and 1980s the host states, facing an influx, pushed many of the boats back into the water and people drowned. Like today, there was a public response to images of people drowning on television and in newspapers. But addressing the issue took political leadership and large-scale international cooperation.

In 1989 under UNHCR leadership, a Comprehensive Plan of Action (CPA) was agreed for Indochinese refugees. It was based on an international agreement for sharing responsibility. The receiving countries in South-East Asia agreed to keep their borders open, engage in search and rescue operations and provide reception to the boat people.

But they did so based on two sets of commitments from other states. First, a coalition of governments – the US, Canada, Australia, New Zealand and the European states – committed to resettle all those who were judged to be refugees. Second, alternative and humane solutions including return and alternative, legal immigration channels were found for those who were not refugees in need of international protection. The CPA led to millions being resettled and the most immediate humanitarian challenge was addressed.

The CPA was not perfect and it is not a perfect analogy to the contemporary Mediterranean, but it highlights the need to a broader framework based on international cooperation and responsibility-sharing. The elements of a solution to the contemporary crisis have to be at a number of different levels.

These include improvements in search and rescue to return to at least the capacity of Mare Nostrum; more equitable burden-sharing and relocation of refugees within the European Union; support to gradually build to protection and human rights capacities of transit countries. In addition to these, creative solutions and additional support are needed for refugee-hosting countries in regions of origin – and we need to promote the refugees' capacities to contribute to their host state. Finally, we need a European resettlement scheme that reflects a commitment to proportionately share responsibility for the global refugee population.

Above all though, solutions have to come from a reaffirmation of the need to uphold asylum and refugee protection, and to see these as a shared global responsibility.

If there is to be a silver lining to the current crisis, it stems from the opportunity to political leadership to reframe how refugees are seen by the public and to come up with creative solutions for refugees and vulnerable migrants on a global scale.

But that will take political courage and leadership.

23 April 2015

⇨ The above information is reprinted with kind permission from *The Conversation*. Please visit www.theconversation.com for further information.

A proper system for sharing the load is the only answer to Europe's migration crisis

Illegal immigration needs to end and the only possible solution is legal immigration – at present we have the worst of all possible worlds.

By Fr. Alexander Lucie-Smith

The recent drowning in the Mediterranean of 900 people is the direct result of British Government policy, says Dan Hodges in a powerful piece on *The Telegraph* website, which I would urge you to read. He certainly makes a case that if the British Government had not withdrawn funding for search and rescue missions, then these 900 refugees would be alive today.

Meanwhile, over at *The Guardian*, there is a strong piece from Richard Ackland, which describes the Australian way of handling the problem of boat people. This is to intercept boats, tow them to somewhere away from Australia, and imprison the migrants in Australian-financed camps, with a view to resettlement outside Australia.

Both policies have one thing in common: they aim to 'discourage' migrants or refugees. If the journey is dangerous and there is no hope of rescue, then perhaps they will not come. If they have no real hope of ever seeing Australia, perhaps they will think twice about attempting entry. And yet, both in the Mediterranean and in Australia, still they come. And across the border from Mexico into the United States too, still they come. Whatever they are trying to get away from is so frightful that the risk of drowning or imprisonment or dying of thirst in the desert is, in their eyes, worth taking.

So, what is to be done? What, one might ask, is the position of the Catholic Church on this matter? What does the Church teach?

Certain bishops' conferences have produced documents on this matter

(such as the bishops of Florida). Our own bishops have this to say in their recent letter about the forthcoming General Election:

'Violence and conflict have led to the massive displacement of people, many of whom seek asylum or refuge. There are also workers and students from overseas who contribute much to the common good of our country. Indeed, most people who settle in this country find work in order to bring up their families and contribute to society's well-being. Immigration is a highly emotive issue and every country needs a policy to control immigration, as well as a positive commitment to policies that facilitate the integration of migrants into the mainstream of society. There is a great danger of blaming immigrants for the ills of society.

We support policies which fairly regulate immigration and uphold the human rights of all, recognising the rights, dignity and protection of refugees and migrants.'

This is interesting for what it says, and for what it does not say.

First of all, it is saying that the British Government is entitled to control immigration. And it is not saying that desperate people from Africa and elsewhere are entitled to come to Britain. But it does use the language of rights to remind us that refugees and immigrants must have their rights and dignity respected.

From a moral point of view the Church is in a dilemma which most people would share: we cannot allow in everyone who wants to come here. At the same time, we cannot carry on as at present, allowing people to

drown. Neither would most of us want to go down the Australian route.

It is a question of balance: the needs of the refugees crossing the Mediterranean balanced against the needs of those who are already here in Britain, which is a relatively small and overcrowded island. Or to put it more dramatically: the needs of those drowning off the coast of Malta, and the needs of the people of Malta, one of the world's smallest and most densely populated countries. It is simply not possible for Malta to absorb thousands of new arrivals. It can't be done. Similarly, it is unlikely that Britain could absorb all the people who wanted to come here, if they were to come. No one can deny that the situation in Syria is catastrophic, but the influx of millions of refugees from there and elsewhere might well be catastrophic for Europe too.

Nor is this alarmist. The influx of Palestinian refugees into Lebanon was a major contributing factor to the Civil War that devastated that country. The amount of refugees in countries that neighbour Syria and Iraq today, such as Jordan, is potentially destabilising.

One thing, though, ought to be clear. The Fortress Europe policy is not working; or, if it were to be made to work, the price would be too high. At the same time, few governments are ever going to admit to their electorates what is blindingly obvious, namely that we must take immigration out of the hands of people smugglers and open up a more generous path to legal entry into Europe.

Does this mean open borders? In all honesty, yes it does, but, and here is the rub, that is what we seem to have already, in that hardly any illegal immigrant is ever deported. A proper guest worker system would be better than the present method of entry through the back door without papers, which is what the clandestini, who number millions, have done in Italy.

Moreover, legalisation and proper enforceable controls would also mean that the immigrants and refugees could be spread more evenly round the continent. At present the burden on a place like Malta is intolerable, as the new arrivals there are forbidden from travelling onwards into the rest of Europe.

At present we have the worst of all possible worlds. Illegal immigration needs to end. The only possible solution is legal immigration, controlled and regulated.

21 April 2015

⇨ The above information is reprinted with kind permission from the Catholic Herald. Please visit www.catholicherald.co.uk for further information.

UN agency becomes first buyer of IKEA's flat-pack refugee shelter

By Kashmira Gander

A UN agency which protects and supports refugees has become the first customer of IKEA's temporary refugee shelter.

The IKEA Foundation, the social arm of the flat-pack Swedish furniture brand, today announced that it will supply 30,000 units of its Better Shelter structure, with 10,000 to be delivered this summer to camps. Over the next three years, the company expects to double or triple production, Reuters reported.

Developed alongside the UN's Refugee Agency (UNHCR), the shelters come in flat-pack cardboard boxes and can be assembled on site without tools.

The 88-square-foot structures sleep five people, and come with a solar panel, a USB outlet and a roof screen that reflects the sun's rays while trapping heat overnight.

During the day, the solar panel charges an LED light, which can be used at night for four hours, or the system can charge a mobile phone.

Refugees are given the structures in two cardboard boxes, which can be assembled in around eight hours with the help of an illustrated manual, Gizmodo reported.

Safety is also considered, as the Better Shelter has a locking door, windows and ventilation, and a photovoltaic system to supply electricity. Each shelter costs $1,150 (£773), and lasts around three years.

Johan Karlsson, the head of business development Better Shelter – part of the firm's social enterprise arm – said the first units will go to house refugees in Iraq and Ethiopia.

'We have around 53.5 million refugees and internal refugees in the world so this of course is just a drop in the ocean,' Jonathan Spampinato, head of strategic planning and communications at Better Shelter told Reuters.

He added: 'Feedback from refugees has been very positive, with the designers receiving useful information.

'Many families, for example, requested the ability to move doors and windows to face relatives and friends, or simply to increase privacy. The designers reconfigured the windows to fit on any panel section of the shelter.'

27 March 2015

⇨ The above information is reprinted with kind permission from *The Independent*. Please visit www.independent.co.uk for further information.

Only a global response can solve Europe's refugee crisis

An article from **The Conversation.**

THE CONVERSATION

By Phil Orchard, Senior Lecturer in Peace and Conflict Studies and International Relations; Research Director at the Asia-Pacific Centre for the Responsibility to Protect at The University of Queensland

The recent deaths of asylum seekers attempting to reach European shores have prompted ongoing calls for action. But, given the scale of the issue, only a comprehensive, global program can go some way to solving the crisis.

The UN High Commissioner for Refugees (UNHCR) notes that more than 366,000 refugees have arrived in Europe by sea so far in 2015. And 80% have come from the world's top ten refugee-producing countries, including half from Syria.

This can be a deadly voyage. The International Organisation for Migration reports that at least 2373 migrants have already died trying to reach Europe this year.

This reflects the immensity of the crisis created by the Syrian conflict. More than four million refugees are now in the countries bordering Syria – Turkey, Lebanon and Jordan – while an estimated 7.6 million are internally displaced within Syria.

An individual country response?

Individual countries have begun to show leadership. This began with German Chancellor Angela Merkel's commitment that Germany would begin processing all asylum seekers who applied on its territory. In so doing, she waived the European Union's (EU) Dublin Regulation, which establishes that asylum seekers must lodge their claim in the first EU country they enter.

Merkel's plan may lead to Germany taking up to 800,000 refugees this year. She laid out her country's response in stark moral terms. She argued that:

Germany is a strong country, we will manage ... If Europe fails on the question of refugees, then it won't be the Europe we wished for.

The UK has reversed its previous position. Prime Minister David Cameron said:

We will do more in providing resettlement for thousands more Syrian refugees.

Prime Minister Tony Abbott has announced that Australia will take a 'significant' number of Syrian refugees beyond the 4500 that it has already pledged to accept.

However, the scale of the crisis means that no single country can deal with it alone. Germany's plan would involve direct EU responsibility for registering and looking after newly arrived refugees in Greece and Italy, as well as creating a common policy on safe countries of origin.

The UNHCR has argued that Europe cannot respond to this crisis 'with a piecemeal or incremental approach'. Instead, it has recommended a mass relocation program with 200,000 places, coupled with improved reception capacities – especially in Greece.

But neither Germany's nor the UNHCR's plan would deal with the main issue: refugees would still have to risk death crossing the Mediterranean Sea to reach Europe to access these programs.

A regional response?

Others argue for a regional response. One suggestion is the creation of a safe zone, which would allow Syrians to remain within the country. Australian Foreign Minister Julie Bishop has echoed this call.

Ethicist Peter Singer has argued that the affluent countries need to provide much more support to the countries supporting large numbers of refugees. Singer also said that sending asylum seekers to safe refugee camps supported by the developed world would eliminate people smuggling.

But these proposals reflect the flipside of the problem: that the world needs to respond to the refugees crossing the Mediterranean and also assist the countries harbouring the bulk of the four million Syrian refugees.

The UNHCR has announced that its budget this year will be 10% less than last year's, while the World Food Programme (WFP) has had to cut the rations being provided to the refugees. The most vulnerable refugees in Lebanon will have only US$13 per month to spend on food, and the WFP may need to cut all assistance to refugees in Jordan.

What's really needed

What is needed, therefore, is a comprehensive, global program. This would include three elements:

1. increased humanitarian assistance to the countries around Syria

2. safe processing centres in Turkey and in either Libya or Tunisia to process asylum claims

3. a global resettlement scheme for refugees and provisions for safe returns for those denied claims.

With respect to humanitarian assistance, the UN Syria Regional Refugee Response Appeal is requesting US$4.5 billion to respond to the situation in Syria and neighbouring countries, but has received only 37% of that total.

This shortfall has been the case since the Syrian conflict began. Most yearly appeals have received

only around 50% of the request funding. This has placed immense pressure on both the international aid agencies responding to the conflict and on the refugee host countries themselves.

A safe processing centre model would serve to deter refugees from crossing the Mediterranean and have the advantage of centrally co-ordinating the processing of individual refugee claims. This, in turn, could:

... enable a fairer distribution of responsibilities among states for providing protection and assistance to refugees.

The UNHCR has noted that such centres could be legal under international law if they clearly reflect the international legal standards – including the UN Refugee Convention and the principle of non-refoulement – and have formal authorisation from host nations. The UNHCR would be the obvious organisation to run the refugee determination process within these centres.

Critically, the centres would need to be safe and agreements would need to be made with the individual host countries. Turkey would likely support such an initiative. Given

the current insecurity in Libya, however, a centre would either need international protection – such as peacekeepers – even with government consent, or alternatively could be established along the border in Tunisia.

But these centres would not work without a clear onward path for processed refugees. The EU is now discussing possible resettlement numbers. Other than the UNHCR's proposed 200,000 figure, European Commission President Jean-Claude Juncker has suggested that individual EU states resettle 120,000 asylum seekers who are currently in Hungary, Greece and Italy. Others have suggested higher figures.

A global commitment to take 400,000 refugees – 10% of the Syrian total – from these processing centres in not unreachable. The model here is the Comprehensive Plan of Action, negotiated in 1989 to respond to the Indochinese boat people. The plan included regional screening for refugees and, while not perfect, resulted in the resettlement of more than 500,000 refugees over six years.

A resettlement scheme could also be combined with a temporary admission process. The EU

already has a temporary protection directive created after the war in Kosovo. That directive allows for refugees to be granted temporary protection in accordance with the Refugee Convention for a period of one year, which can be extended.

Given the nature of the Syrian war, a longer protection period would be warranted.

By combining these three approaches, individual countries would have the opportunity either to commit to refugee resettlement or to fund the centres' humanitarian operation and costs – or both. Most importantly, these approaches would significantly increase the burden-sharing between the refugee-hosting countries near Syria and the rest of the developed world.

7 September 2015

⇨ The above information is reprinted with kind permission from *The Conversation*. Please visit www.theconversation.com for further information.

Key facts

⇨ In 2014, there were 19.5 million refugees around the world, including 5.1 million Palestinian refugees. According to the UN Refugee Agency, the leading countries of origin for refugees in 2014 were:

- Syria: 3.88 million

- Afghanistan: 2.59 million

- Somalia: 1.1 million (page 1)

⇨ During 2013, some 1.1 million individual applications for asylum or refugee status were submitted to governments and UNHCR offices. (page 1)

⇨ With 109,600 asylum claims, Germany was for the first time since 1999 the world's largest recipient of new individual applications, followed by the United States of America (84,400) and South Africa (70,000). (page 1-2)

⇨ In 2014, global displacement reached historic levels: 59.5 million people were forced to flee their homes: roughly the same number of people as in Britain. If these people made up their own country, it would be the 24th largest nation in the world. (page 6)

⇨ In 2014 alone, 8.3 million people were forced to flee: the highest annual increase on record. (page 6)

⇨ That means that 42,500 people were forced to leave their homes every day because of conflict or persecution. (page 6)

⇨ Of these people, 19.5 million are refugees, 1.8 million are asylum seekers and 38.2 million were internally displaced within their own country. (page 6)

⇨ The top five host countries for refugees are:

- Turkey

- Pakistan

- Lebanon

- Iran

- Ethiopia. (page 6)

⇨ 11% of respondents would agree to take a refugee into their home for six months. (page 6)

⇨ More than 25,000 unaccompanied children lodged asylum applications in 77 countries last year, a fraction of the number of displaced minors across the globe. (page 8)

⇨ By the end of last year (2013), 2.5 million Syrians had fled across the country's borders and 6.5 million were internally displaced – more than 40% of the population. (page 8)

⇨ The UK immigration detention estate is one of the largest in Europe. From 2009 until the end of 2013, between 2,000 and 3,500 migrants have been in detention at any given time. (page 13)

⇨ Over 1,000 children were detained for the purpose of immigration control in 2009, and this number was reduced to just under 130 in 2011. It rose to 240 in 2012, before falling to 228 in 2013 with the majority detained at the Cedars pre-departure accommodation facility, opened in September 2011. (page 13)

⇨ In late 2014 the estimated average cost of detention was £97 per day. (page 13)

⇨ 34 women disclosed the experiences in their home countries which led them to seek asylum in the UK:

- 19 women said that they had been raped, 21 women had experienced other sexual violence and 24 altogether – over 70% of the 34 who answered – had experienced either rape or sexual violence. Eight had been raped by soldiers, police or prison guards.

- 28 women said that they had experienced gender-related persecution under the headings we asked about – rape, sexual violence, forced marriage, forced prostitution or female genital mutilation.

- 21 women said that they had been tortured, and 26 altogether said they had experienced either rape or torture. (page 19)

⇨ So far in 2015, nearly 1,000 asylum seekers have drowned (April 2015). (page 28)

⇨ Since the start of the crisis, Handicap International's 450-strong team has helped over 180,000 people in Syria. (page 30)

⇨ Almost four million people displaced from Syria have registered with the UN High Commissioner for refugees. The burden has fallen almost entirely on the shoulders of neighbouring states, who host 95% of the refugees. In Lebanon, one in five people is a Syrian refugee, the equivalent per capita of the UK hosting nearly 13 million refugees. (page 32)

Asylum application

If a person wishes to stay in the UK as a refugee, they must apply for asylum. To be eligible they must have left their country and be unable to go back because they fear persecution. Refugees should apply for asylum as soon as they arrive in the UK.

Asylum seeker

The refugee council defines an asylum seeker as 'a person who has left their country of origin and formally applied for asylum in another country but whose application has not yet been concluded.'

Azure payment card

Given to people who have been refused asylum in the UK, and so are unable to work, but cannot return home. The card is pre-loaded with £35.39 a week to buy food and essentials.

Detained fast track

The Refugee Council says that 'the fast track procedure is used to determine asylum applications from people who the Home Office assesses to be "suitable". Applicants in the detained fast track are held at an Immigration Removal Centre and the initial decision on their case and any appeals happen at a faster pace than in the community. A case is considered suitable for the fast track process where it appears to the Home Office that the asylum claim can be decided "quickly".'

Detention centre

A centre used for the short-term detention of illegal immigrants and refugees.

Economic migrant

Someone who has chosen to move to another country in order to work. Refugees are not economic migrants.

Internationally displaced person

Someone who has fled their home but remains within their own country.

International Humanitarian Law (IHL)

A set of rules and principles that govern armed conflict. IHL protects refugees from States that are involved in armed conflict.

The Jungle (Calais)

The nickname given to a series of refugee camps that were set up near Calais, France, inhabited by migrants and refugees trying to reach the UK.

Overstayer

A person who was permitted to stay in the UK for a limited period of time and who has remained longer than this time.

Refugee

A person who has left their home country and cannot return because they fear that they will be persecuted on the grounds of race, religion, nationality, political affiliation or social group. In the UK a person is officially known as a refugee when they claim asylum and this claim is accepted by the Government.

Refugee camp

A camp that provides shelter/temporary housing for refugees or displaced persons. The world's largest refugee camp is Dadaab in Kenya. The camp hosts 35,000 people in five camps.

Statelessness

Statelessness refers to a lack of nationality, which can occur because of the redrawing of borders, or holes in nationality laws.

United Nations High Commissioner for Refugees (UNHCR)

The Office of the United Nations High Commissioner for Refugees was established in 1950 and aims to 'lead and coordinate international action to protect refugees and resolve refugee problems worldwide.'

Assignments

Brainstorming

⇨ In small groups, discuss what you know about refugees. Consider the following:

- What is the definition of a refugee?

- What's the different between a refugee and a migrant?

- Why do people become refugees?

- Do you think the general attitude towards refugees in the UK is currently positive or negative?

Research

⇨ Research the asylum process in the UK and, in small groups, discuss your findings and whether you believe the process is fair.

⇨ Research the movement of refugees after the Second World War and write some notes that explore your findings. Share your notes with the rest of your class.

⇨ Read the article *UN agency becomes first buyer of IKEA's flat-pack refugee shelter* on page 37 and conduct some research into other ingenious inventions or schemes that aim to help refugees.

Design

⇨ Create a leaflet that answers the following questions:

- Who is an internally displaced person?

- Who is a stateless person?

- What is an asylum seeker?

⇨ Choose one of the articles in this book and create an illustration to highlight the key themes/ messages of your chosen article.

⇨ Create a poster that illustrates the facts from the article on page seven *Asylum trends 2014*.

Oral

⇨ Choose one of the illustrations from this book and, in pairs, discuss why the artist decided to depict the themes they did.

⇨ In pairs, discuss your views on detention centres for refugees. Look at the article *Immigration detention in the UK* on page 13 for further information.

⇨ 'The Azure card for refuges asylum seekers is a very practical solution and £35 a week should be plenty for one person to live on.' Debate this motion as a class.

⇨ In small groups, discuss why you think so many migrants/refugees are willing to risk death in the Mediterranean in order to reach Europe. Read the article *Risking death in the Mediterranean: the least bad option for so many migrants* on page 28 to help inform your discussion.

Reading/writing

⇨ 'What are the main reasons people become refugees? What other reasons drive people from their homes?' Answer this question with no more than one side of A4.

⇨ Write a diary entry from the point of view of a refugee living in either:

- a detention centre in the UK

- a refugee camp in Syria

⇨ Choose two newspapers and, over the course of a week, cut out all the articles that talk about refugees/migrants. At the end of the week write one-paragraph answers to the following questions:

- Are the terms, 'refugee' and 'migrant' used correctly in the articles you have seen?

- Is press coverage largely positive or negative?

- What are the key issues identified?

⇨ Watch the 2004 film *The Terminal*, starring Tom Hanks, and write an essay exploring the theme of statelessness throughout the film.

⇨ Write a blog post that will raise awareness of disabled refugees.

⇨ Using the articles in chapter three, identify some of the proposed solutions to the refugee crisis and summarise these in a piece for your school newspaper.

Acknowledgements

The publisher is grateful for permission to reproduce the material in this book. While every care has been taken to trace and acknowledge copyright, the publisher tenders its apology for any accidental infringement or where copyright has proved untraceable. The publisher would be pleased to come to a suitable arrangement in any such case with the rightful owner.

Images
All images courtesy of iStock. Icon on page 41 courtesy of Flaticon.

Illustrations
Don Hatcher: pages 8 & 30. Simon Kneebone: pages 14 & 29. Angelo Madrid: pages 3 & 36.

Additional acknowledgements
Editorial on behalf of Independence Educational Publishers by Cara Acred.

With thanks to the Independence team: Mary Chapman, Sandra Dennis, Christina Hughes, Jackie Staines and Jan Sunderland.

Cara Acred

Cambridge

September 2015